C000163947

## ...er Comments

"...ue in a beach-side Catholic church is the ... from Washington, D.C. Drawing from ...s, vital statistics, and published histories, The Battle of Turkey Thicket follows Philip Thomas Hughes from an orphanage to the battlefields of a Cold War suddenly turned hot. Christopher Russell's easy writing style creates a vivid collage of mid-20th century America, Japan, and Korea."

**Susanne Hagan Coffey**
**University of North Texas**

"This is a bittersweet story of an American life lost in a war forgotten by most yet still to be resolved. It is a primer for what it was like to become a post WWII soldier, go to war in Korea, and hold the Pusan Perimeter until the rest of us got there. The journey from Brookland to Arlington is Private Hughes's story. His life is worth remembering and through him honoring all who died in Korea. Mr. Russell's book does that admirably."

**1st Lt. Robert W. Ricker**
**U.S. Army, Korean War veteran**
**2nd Ordnance Medium Maintenance Co 8th Army**

"Christopher Russell's story about the life and times of Philip Thomas Hughes – an adopted child and eventual runaway – offers a vivid portrait of life in Washington, D.C. after World War II. His description of the first months of the Korean War is fast-paced, detailed, and deeply disconcerting. The Battle of Turkey Thicket is the poignant story of an almost Unknown Soldier."

**Michael Collier**
**Director, Breadloaf Writer's Conference**
**Poet Laureate of Maryland, 2001-2004**

"The Battle of Turkey Thicket is an extraordinarily well researched account of the life of a young orphan whose difficult childhood eventually drove him to a forsaken part of South Korea in 1950 where he was killed by communist forces from the north during their aggressive invasion. The author's description of the battles in which Private Hughes was engaged drives home the futility of the delaying action attempted by the U.S. Army in the early days of the Korean War."

**Lieutenant Colonel Edward De Santis**
**U.S. Army (Retired)**

"The Battle of Turkey Thicket is the true story of two adopted boys seeking their identity and place in life. Without this perceptive and captivating work, Philip Hughes would just be another forgotten casualty of the forgotten war."

**Vincent B. Bennett Jr.**
**Captain, United States Air Force (Retired)**

# THE BATTLE OF
# TURKEY THICKET

# THE BATTLE OF
# TURKEY THICKET

The Journeys of an
Orphan, Altar Boy, Runaway, and
Teenage Soldier from Washington, D.C.

By Christopher Russell

Baltimore, Maryland

Cover photo: 1951. Three members to the 25th Infantry Division's 24th Regiment assist a wounded colleague's withdrawal from the battlefield south of Chorwon, Korea. *Photo by Tom Nebbia for the U.S. Army.*

Cover design and title page photo by Christopher Russell.

Text editor: Jeanette DiLouie

First Printing: 2017
ISBN 978-0-9990983-2-5
Library of Congress Control Number: 2017909345

Baritone Books
Baltimore, Maryland
www.baritonebooks.com

"Pray for all the boys who were killed."

*Philip Thomas Hughes,*
*August 29, 1950*

# ABOUT THE AUTHOR

Christopher Russell enjoys the irresistible evidence of history where ever it is found. He lives in the Baltimore area with his wife and daughter in a 1915-vintage house that provides joy in excess of the do-it-yourself attention it demands.

The author's ongoing research of the Korean War era and its impact can be found online at turkeythicket.blogspot.com.

# Table of Contents

# Acknowledgements & Bibliography

**Frank Hughes** is at the top of this list. Frank, his wife Cici, and daughter Kathleen welcomed and facilitated the research that made this story possible. I am very grateful to them. More on their contribution in the epilogue.

**Bevin Alexander.** 1986. *Korea: The First War We Lost.* Hippocrene Books, New York. The discussion of romantic intimacies experienced by American soldiers in Japan is derived from portions of this text.

**Roy Appleman.** 1961. *South to the Naktong, North to the Yalu.* Center of Military History, United States Army. This text is the classic Korean War history as promulgated by the U.S. Army. Aside from describing key events and personalities, this book provides most of the battle maps included here.

**Department of the Army**. March 21, 1951. *Mess Management.* TM 10-402. Washington: GPO. Everything you wanted to know about food preparation for Korean War-era combat troops.

**Hal Barker.** The Korean War Project. Mr. Barker maintains a superlative website that includes a searchable database of U.S. military personnel who lost their lives in Korea. www.koreanwar.org.

*The New American Bible.* 1988. Macmillan, Inc. Benziger Publishing Company, Mission Hills, California.

**William T. Bowers, et. al.** 1996. *Black Soldier, White Army: The 24th Infantry Regiment in Korea.* Center of Military history, United States Army. A source of statistics, maps, and a discussion of occupation duty in Japan.

**Professor Kim Brandt.** *Learning from Babysan.* Blog essay hosted by the Japan Society. Comprehensive discussion of the cultural dynamics of fraternization in occupied Japan. http://aboutjapan.japansociety.org/learning-from-babysan.

**Russell Brines.** *The Washington Evening Star.* September 11, 1950. "American Artillery Knocks Out Many Red Guns in Taegu Duel; South Koreans Advance in East." Describes the no-man's land west of Hill 300.

**Lynnita Jean Brown.** Founder of the Korean War Educator website. Among other items, this website provides memoirs of men and women who served in uniform during the Korean War. www.koreanwar-educator.org.

**Rev. William Cocco** and the office staff of St. Edmond's Catholic Church in Rehoboth Beach generously copied pages from the parish register.

**Raymond C. Colton, Sr.** 2003. *Sacrificial Lambs: 24th Division Korea July 1950.* Ivy House Publishing Group, Raleigh, North Carolina. Memoir of a U.S. Army soldier whose time-in-service closely paralleled that of Philip Hughes.

**Anna Cook.** 2012. *Humanizing the Enemy.* Florida State University honors thesis. An evaluation of the social dynamics of interaction between Americans and the Japanese during the post-war occupation. http://diginole.lib.fsu.edu/islandora/object/fsu:204543/datastream/PDF/view

**William F. Dean.** 1954. *General Dean's Story.* Greenwood Press, Publishers. Westport, Connecticut.

**Lt. Colonel Edward De Santis, U.S. Army (Ret.)** provided thorough fact checking of the army-related terminology regarding weapons, gear, and inspections protocol.

**Connie DiPasquale.** *A History of the Orphan Trains.* University of Kansas. http://www.kancoll.org/articles/orphans/or_hist.htm.

**G. N. Donovan.** 1952. *Use of Infantry Weapons and Equipment in Korea.* Technical Memorandum ORO-T-18 (FEC). Operations Research Office. The Johns Hopkins University, Chevy Chase, Maryland. Insight on the use (or misuse) of weapons and equipment in the field, plus the part about survival rates in battle.

**Megan B. Dwyer** of the National Archives at College Park replied to my correspondence by sending photocopies of documents from the unit records of the 19th Infantry Regiment for 26 August through 28 September 1950.

**Brig. Gen. Uzal W. Ent, U.S. Army (Ret.).** 1996. *Fighting on the Brink: Defense of the Pusan Perimeter.* Turner Publishing Company, Padukah, Kentucky. By inserting his own additional research, Gen. Ent effectively re-wrote Roy Appleman's *South to the Naktong, North to the Yalu.* The most definitive source for determining Philip Hughes's battle itinerary in Korea.

**Familysearch.org.** A searchable database of census records, border crossings, steamship passenger rosters, passport applications, birth certificates, military draft registrations, and more.

**John J. Feeley, Jr. and Rosie Dempsey.** 2011. *Brookland.* Acadia Publishing, Charleston, South Carolina. One of those wonderful sepia-toned, soft cover books with a collection of vintage photos.

**Findagrave.com.** Online, searchable database of gravesites.

**Carlton Fletcher.** *Glover Park History* – a web blog. This posting provides a detailed history of Washington, D.C.'s Industrial Home School. http://gloverparkhistory.com/institutions-cemeteries/institutions/former-institutions/brief-history-of-the-industrial-home-school/.

**David Halberstam.** 2007. *The Coldest Winter: America and the Korean War.* Hyperion, New York. A fascinating study of the leaders and tricky leadership dynamics that precipitated the Korean War and shaped its conduct.

**Major Thomas E. Hanson.** 2006. *America's First Cold War Army: Combat Readiness in the Eighth U.S. Army, 1949-1950.* Ohio State University. This is a Ph.D. dissertation that describes the issues faced by the Army occupation units in Japan immediately prior to the Korean War.

**Ralph Derr Harrity.** 2005. *Q Clan: The First Summer of the Korean Conflict, June–September 1950, A Lieutenant's Memoir.* Dorrance Publishing Company, Pittsburgh. Mr. Harrity's service in Korea very often put him in the vicinity of Philip Hughes. Drawn from a meticulous diary, his book provides gritty details about the Kum River Line, Taejon, and Kyongju. He regularly noted prevailing weather conditions. His memoir provides poignant observations about the Korean War's impact on soldiers and civilians alike.

**Merry Helm.** 2014. *Prairie Boys at War: Korea: Volume I: June – October 1950,* Prairie Boy Books. Ms. Helm, historian of the 24th Infantry Division Association, kindly shared scanned images of the division's "Order of Battle Journal," covering the summer and fall of 1950.

**Marguerite Higgins.** 1951. *War in Korea: The Report of a Woman Combat Correspondent.* Doubleday & Company, Inc., New York. Plucky little Maggie Higgins managed by sheer force of will to reach the front lines of the Korean War in its initial days. She provides much of the story of Philip Hughes's battalion commander, Lt. Col. Harold "Red" Ayres.

**Col. Bruce Hock, U.S. Army (Ret.)** graciously answered my questions about the duties accruing to various ranks in the Army.

**Bill Hume.** 1953. *Babysan: A Private Look at the Japanese Occupation.* Kasuga Boeki K.K., Tokyo, Japan. Once dubbed "the Navy's most talented serviceman" by Yank magazine, Bill Hume (1916-2009) was among other things a gifted illustrator. A U.S. Navy reservist recalled in 1951 for service in Japan, he published a truly fascinating compendium of his cartoon illustrations depicting the cultural interface between American military men and their Japanese girlfriends.

(Unknown Byline). *The Indianapolis Star.* January 24, 1909. "Girls from Convent School Attend Indianapolis Theaters." Describes the wholesome adventures of Wilhelmina Knue and her Oldenburg Academy classmates.

**E.J. Kahn, Jr.** 1952. *The Peculiar War: Impressions of a Reporter in Korea.* Random House, New York. This *New Yorker* magazine author wrote poignant observations about the Korean people, cities, and landscape amid war.

**Wyatt Kingseed.** June 2004. *American History.* "The 'Bonus Army' War in Washington. http://www.historynet.com

**Donald Knox.** 1981. *The Korean War: An Oral History.* Harcourt, Inc. A compendium of interviews with veterans of the Korean War's first year.

**Luke Macaulay.** 2005. *Passing from Memory – An Analysis of American Servicemen's Letters: Korea 1950-1953.* University of Glasgow. A thorough discussion of the logistics and human impact of correspondence sent to and from military personnel serving in Korea.

**Robert Malesky.** *Bygone Brookland: Tales from a Storied Neighborhood.* bygonebrookland.com

**Col. John D. Martz, Jr.** May/June 1954. *Homeward Bound.* "Quartermaster Review." A detailed description of all that was involved in Korean War graves registration – that is, retrieval of those fallen in battle. U.S. Army Quartermaster Foundation.

**Dr. Michael McKee,** a commissioned officer of the U.S. Army during the early 1960s, kindly allowed an email dialogue in which he explained the division of labor across officer ranks in an infantry context. He also explained the administrivia involved when a soldier travels domestically. Finally, Mike conducted a thoughtful review of this book's draft, offering a vigorous "reality check" especially on the military tactics described here.

**Carole Merritt.** 2008. *Something So Horrible: The Springfield Race Riot of 1908.* Abraham Lincoln Presidential Library Foundation, Springfield, Illinois. https://www.illinois.gov/alplm/museum/Learning/Documents/Race_Riot_Ca talog_2008.pdf.

**Donna Noelken,** Archives Specialist, granted me a security clearance for my access to microfilm records of Korean War-era morning reports at the National Personnel Records Center, U.S. National Archives in St. Louis, Missouri.

**Adam Novotny.** This remarkable young man provides patient and cheerful tutelage on all matters of faith. He's one text message away.

**Lt. Col. Dean A. Nowowiejski.** 2001. *Comrades in Arms: The Influence of George S. Patton on Walton H. Walker's Pusan Perimeter Defense.* U.S. Army War College, Carlisle Barracks, Pennsylvania. A critique of General Walker's command and management style, derived in part from first-hand recollections of his Korean War staff.

**Melinda L. Pash.** 2012. *In the Shadow of the Greatest Generation: The Americans Who Fought the Korean War.* New York University Press Books. In contrast to formal military histories, Professor Pash's work describes the American soldier's Korean War experience, from recruitment through discharge and collection of benefits.

**Sgt. Lloyd W. Pate, with B. J. Cutler.** 1955. *Reactionary!* Harper & Brothers Publishers, New York. This is the only first-person account written by someone who served in the same unit (King Company, 19th Infantry Regiment) as Philip Hughes. While Philip was not mentioned in this book, it gives valuable details about the activity on Hill 300.

**John Clagett Proctor.** May 26, 1946. *The Washington Sunday Star.* "Historic St. Ann's Infant Asylum." Page 16.

**R.W. "Bill" Rowland** lived in the Washington, D.C. area for much of his adult life. He enlisted in the Army in 1946, then served with the Signal Corps while on occupation duty in Japan. He kindly shared his recollections of the recruiting center in downtown D.C. and his shipboard travel across the Pacific.

**The staff** of the Rehoboth Beach Public Library were very engaging and quite helpful in pointing me toward microfilm records of the *Delaware Coast Press*, which featured obituaries for Tom and Wilhelmina Hughes.

**Joe Sweeney.** 1998. *The Dead, the Missing, and the Captured.* 24th Infantry Division Association. Mr. Sweeney made a near-definitive roster of Korean War casualties suffered by the 19th Infantry Regiment.

(Unknown byline). *Time* Magazine. July 24, 1950. "War: The Land and the People." An essay describing the geography, demographics, economy, flora, and fauna of Korea.

(Unknown byline). *Time* Magazine. July 31, 1950. "Battle of Korea: Retreat from Taejon." Describes the action and subsequent consequences of the debacle in Taejon.

(Unknown byline). *Time* Magazine. August 14, 1950. "War: The First Team." An article describing the U.S. Marines' arrival in Korea.

(Unknown byline). *Time* Magazine. September 4, 1950. "Battle of Korea: Glorious Pages." A rumination on the war's conduct on the Pusan Perimeter.

(Unknown byline). *Time* Magazine. September 18, 1950. "Battle of Korea: Sagging Roof." An update on the war's progress on the Pusan Perimeter. The first *Time* article on the Korean War published after Philip Hughes's death.

(Unknown byline). *The Washington Post*. September 26, 1950. "GI Killed Who Asked Prayers for Others." Page 5. Article announcing the death of Philip Hughes, including his mother's observations.

(Unknown byline). *The Washington Evening Star*. October 24, 1939. "Chest-Aided St. Ann's Gives Children of Poverty a Chance." Page 2.

(Unknown byline). *The Washington Sunday Star*. October 6, 1946. "St. Ann's Asylum Babies Move from 120-Year-Old Building." Page A-14.

(Unknown byline). *The Washington Evening Star*. September 25, 1950. "'Worst is Over,' D.C. Youth Says in Final Letter." Page 22.

(Unknown byline). *The Washington Evening Star*. September 26, 1950. "3 General Hospitals to be Reopened to Care for Wounded." Page 1.

(Unknown byline). *The Washington Evening Star*. December 31, 1950. "War-Widow Mother Notified of Death of Son in Korea." Page 14. This pertains to Marie Stevenson, mother of Charles Leroy Stevenson. Mrs. Stevenson's husband, Charles Sr., succumbed in 1929 to lingering ailments inflicted during his service in World War I.

*The Washington Evening Star*. February 25, 1952. Obituary for Philip Thomas Hughes. Page 14.

**Donald Wulfinghoff** has been a stalwart mentor through the years, most recently with respect to publication of this book. See Don's work at www.energybooks.com.

**David T. Zabecki.** May 1, 2009. *Military History*. "Stand or Die – 1950: Defense of Korea's Pusan Perimeter."

**Jeannette DiLouie** wrestled my draft to the ground, hog-tied it, and ensured that the final product became a tasty barbeque. I highly recommend her personalized, thoughtful service. Please visit: www.innovativeediting.com.

# Preface

The American landscape is generously sprinkled with commemorative markers and plaques of all kinds. Displayed on buildings, bridges, and roadside posts, each is an attempt to immortalize a fleeting human experience. Creating these commemorative artifacts was very much a 20th-century phenomenon. It was a time before the advent of websites, when wealth and significance were embodied in the steel and masonry of tangible property. A flood of good intentions ensured a proliferation of these signs, so that their sheer number renders any one of them unremarkable. We may repeatedly encounter the same marker for years and never totally absorb its message. The impact of these memorials tends to diminish as time passes and on-lookers become increasingly indifferent.

One such plaque is found in St. Edmond's Catholic Church, which is located just a block from the boardwalk of Rehoboth Beach, Delaware. This particular memorial bears a starkly understated inscription:

1932 – 1950
IN MEMORIAM
PHILIP THOMAS HUGHES
PRIVATE UNITED STATES ARMY
KILLED IN KOREA 9-12-50

This was obviously sponsored by a church benefactor. Yet its inconspicuous placement in the chapel relegates it to virtual irrelevance. The plaque has been there for so long that an inquiry to the parish office in 2014 found no one who could comment on its origin.

Anyone who cares to read this plaque knows straight away that it honors a teenage boy. Yet the inscription imparts a compound injustice. This kid lost his life. He did so in a war that has become obscured by indifference. So too has the little plaque devoted to his memory.

There is an epic story behind that plaque in St. Edmond's Church. It begins with Philip's family and the community from which he longed to escape. Then, in recounting Philip's journeys, we witness the civic evolution of Washington, D.C., the societal reconstruction of Japan after World War II, and the chaotic battlefields of the Korean War.

At the same time, the story of Philip and his family is one of spiritual faith that was formed, challenged, and reconstituted through sacrifice.

What follows is a factual history. At the very least, it is an attempt to rescue the identity of Philip Thomas Hughes – and the story of his journeys – from oblivion.

# Prologue

## THE BONUS ARMY

Seventeen thousand American veterans of World War I converged on Washington, D.C. during the spring of 1932, at the height of the Great Depression. Traveling by car, freight train, or thumbed rides, the once victorious doughboys of the American Expeditionary Force were now in their 30s and 40s. Their singular goal was for Congress to immediately redeem the $1,000 certificates awarded to each veteran in 1924 as promissory notes intended for redemption in 1945.

Clever newspapermen dubbed these veterans the "Bonus Expeditionary Force," or for short, the "Bonus Army." Led by Walter W. Waters, a 34-year-old unemployed fruit cannery superintendent from Oregon, the Bonus Army enjoyed widely popular support, including the public endorsement of retired Marine Major General Smedley Butler, a two-time recipient of the Congressional Medal of Honor.

That any of the veterans would live to see the "Tombstone Bonus" of 1945 was increasingly in doubt. Perhaps 20 percent of them were disabled, and many more were undernourished or simply in dubious health. All were made desperate by the worsening economy. Their petitions mailed to Congress since 1930 were met with indifference. A show of numbers on the doorstep of the Capitol, the veterans felt, would influence legislators to grant their wish.

Family members accompanied many of the veterans because they had nothing else to occupy themselves. Numerous camp followers with other agendas mingled with the veterans, including alleged "communist agitators." While predating the advent of visual news media, the gathering of the Bonus Army was a forerunner of the iconic civil rights marches taking place some 30 years later.

The Bonus Army's number swelled to about 26,000 souls by the end of May, adding another nine percent to Washington, D.C.'s regular population. It organized several squatters' campsites in the city, with its forward base being a block of abandoned buildings on Pennsylvania Avenue just west of the Capitol. The veterans' largest settlement, which included whole families, sprouted opposite the Washington Navy Yard on the muddy, eastern banks of the Anacostia River. Their camp was dubbed the "Bonus City." It was much like any other "Hooverville" created by families made homeless by the Depression. Occupants built their own dwellings from scrap lumber, tarpaper, corrugated tin, and other scavenged materials.

So committed were they to their encampment that the veterans organized their impromptu garrison with street names and rudimentary sanitation facilities. And just as they had done to pass the time in France in 1919 while waiting their turn for a homebound ocean crossing, the veterans conducted daily drill formations and parades.

Anticipating the House of Representatives' June 15 vote on the Wright Patman Bonus Bill, the veterans from Bonus City marched across the 11th Street Bridge, through the Washington Navy Yard, past the Marine Barracks, and up Pennsylvania Avenue. They gathered in orderly fashion on the grounds and steps of the U.S. Capitol Building, armed only with signs announcing their home states.

The House vote was in their favor. Two days later, however, the Senate refused to endorse the bill, voting 62 to 18 against it. Legislative failure did not bring an end to the standoff. Would Congress introduce a follow-up bill?

Many veterans had no homes to which they could return. "Stick it out" became their mantra through the hot days of June and July. To then-President Herbert Hoover, the continued encampment was a conspicuous and embarrassing indictment of his administration's handling of America's economic malaise. He directed the military to prepare contingencies for clearing the Bonus Army from the nation's capital.

This task was entrusted to General Douglas MacArthur, son of a decorated Civil War veteran, and himself a veteran officer of the First World War and architect of his own, growing legend. MacArthur's troops practiced anti-riot tactics at Fort Myer, just across the Potomac.

At 10:00 a.m. on Thursday, July 28, the Metropolitan Police spearheaded a sharp initial encounter seeking to evict about 200 veterans from their forward base on Pennsylvania Avenue. Frayed nerves yielded to gunfire, which claimed the lives of two veterans. At 2:55 p.m., MacArthur ordered his ranks to close in.

July 28, 1932. Washington, D.C. Metropolitan Police confront World War I veterans encamped on federal property. *U.S. Army.*

Down Pennsylvania Avenue came 1,000 infantry with fixed bayonets, plus horse-mounted cavalry with support totaling perhaps another thousand men. Accompanying this force was a squad of six tanks under the command of Major George S. Patton. Some of the veterans recognized the clattering armor to be Renault FTs left over from the Great War's Western Front.

Government workers turned out to watch the military converge on the Capitol. At first, they cheered the Army, believing the advance was a parade of support for the bonus seekers. But to the onlookers' shock, the troops began lobbing the beleaguered veterans with cans of adamsite gas, which emitted a vomit-inducing agent. Starkly reminded of the Kaiser's use of mustard gas in France, most of the veterans were too stunned to offer any meaningful resistance. They retreated southward across the 11th Street Bridge to the Anacostia Flats.

At the other end of Pennsylvania Avenue, the White House received a stream of updates as events unfolded. President Hoover wanted to claim victory and suspend the deployment of troops as quickly as possible, hoping to minimize negative publicity. Hoover ordered MacArthur to stand down in an order issued through Secretary of War Hurley.

MacArthur chose to ignore this order. Viscerally incensed by the Bonus Army's alleged communist element, MacArthur ordered his forces south across the 11th Street bridge to close on the larger encampment in Anacostia. Occupants, including women and children, were given an hour to vacate. Soldiers advanced on the camp, torching the shanty structures. The dispersed campers flooded the roads out of the city. The Bonus Army was no more.

On July 28, 1932, within sight of the U.S. Capitol, Douglas MacArthur got the victory he craved, not on a battlefield, but through what was essentially a police action, achieved at the expense of his fellow veterans.

History would have more to say about MacArthur.

About a month later, just a few blocks from the Capitol, the infant who would become Philip Thomas Hughes was born to a mother who either could not – or would not – care for him.

Eighteen years later, in 1950, Douglas MacArthur would orchestrate another "police action," this time across the globe in the far-east Asian nation of Korea. No one knew that Philip would be among the over 34,000 American lives claimed by hostile action there. Nor did anyone realize that General MacArthur and these two police actions would provide the bookends for Philip's life story.

# CHAPTER 1

# Introduction

Turkey Thicket is a relatively open space in the otherwise densely developed residential community of Brookland, which is located in the northeast quadrant of Washington, D.C. Reasons for the area's name are not clear, since no known documentation ascribes to it an abundance of wild turkeys or, for that matter, a thicket.

For a time during the Civil War, Turkey Thicket hosted an encampment of Union soldiers, yet it saw no clash of armies. Still, a very real battle began there some 80 years later, in a row house that still stands today along its periphery, just a couple blocks north of the Catholic University of America.

It was in this home during the late 1940s that two teenage boys challenged the will of their adoptive mother in a conflict that precipitated a fateful yet redemptive journey.

The Battle of Turkey Thicket would rage across state lines, from Washington, D.C. to Chicago's Skid Row. It spilled across the border into Canada. It reached its climax during the darkest days of a war in Korea, on a place that the U.S. Army called "Hill 300." It was in the shadow of that hill in 1950 that the elder brother, Philip Hughes, was killed in action not two weeks past his 18th birthday.

Time has almost erased the identity of Philip Thomas Hughes. Public records provide a few scant milestones describing his life and times. His surviving kid brother, now in his eighties, adds only scattered memories.

Philip's most tangible legacies are inscriptions found on his tombstone and on a plaque bolted to the interior wall of a beachside church. Yet the few remaining threads of Philip's identity weave a unique tapestry – stories about a Catholic family and its use of church institutions, an increasingly forgotten cultural niche in the nation's capital, and the Cold War's harrowing flashpoint in Korea.

By stitching together Philip Hughes's story, we can learn not only about the curious adventure of his life and the war that took it, but also about the world from which he yearned to escape.

Official records provide Wednesday, August 31, 1932 as his date of birth. The veracity of that date, as well as the identity of his birth parents, are probably confirmed in the records of a Washington, D.C. orphans' asylum now archived by the Catholic University of America. Since access to these archives is highly restricted, there was no attempt to view those records for the compilation of this history.

Philip was adopted as a toddler by a childless, middle-aged couple from Indiana. His adoptive father was a trade union executive, newly transplanted to Washington, D.C. Philip enjoyed a comfortable if not privileged childhood, in a city bursting with economic energy during the Great Depression and Second World War.

This charmed life quickly unraveled, however. Philip in his teen years transformed from altar boy to runaway, and from reform school truant to army inductee. While only 17 years old, Philip crossed the Pacific Ocean to join the American occupation forces garrisoned in post-war Japan. It was from there that he and many other boy soldiers were hurriedly shoveled into that meat grinder that was the Korean War.

Because Korea was the first war from which deceased American combatants were repatriated en masse from foreign soil, his remains rest today in Arlington National Cemetery, only a few miles from where he grew up.

We would like to think that Philip, like any American soldier, was sacrificed for a reason. *Mother, God, and country* are the traditional rationale. But if this applies to Philip Hughes, it does so only in a twisted way.

Seen differently, his sacrifice has very specific meaning. A full recounting of his story documents the Battle of Turkey Thicket and its most enduring outcome.

# CHAPTER 2

# Washington, D.C.

Because he was adopted by a couple living in Washington, D.C., it is likely that Philip was born in or near that city. If so, chances are that Philip's birth parents resided in the same area. His identity was in a sense derived from the demographic, civic, and historic attributes that shaped community life in the nation's capital during the years leading up to 1932.

Consider first the location and function of the city itself. *Washington, District of Columbia* was chosen to be the capital of the United States as a result of the U.S. Congress's Residence Act of 1790, which reflected a political compromise between northern and southern states. The result was a 10-square mile federal district carved out of the states of Maryland and Virginia, straddling the Potomac River.

While the geographic heart of the District was where the Anacostia River emptied into the Potomac on its eastern bank on the Maryland side, the city was largely undeveloped at its inception and would grow slowly through the early 1800s. Its boundaries contained the tobacco ports of Georgetown, then in Maryland, and Alexandria, Virginia, with the balance consisting of farmland. The capital city would have to be built from scratch, per the plan drafted by French city planner Pierre L'Enfant in 1791.

Events leading up to the U.S. Civil War (1861-1865) brought great change to the City of Washington. First, the District lost a third of its land area in 1846 when Alexandria residents successfully petitioned to take back the former Virginia portion of the city. The advent of war spawned massive bureaucratic expansion, which drove much of the city's population growth of

75 percent between 1860 and 1870. This boom fostered tremendous construction, not only of offices, but also for homes, commerce, and utility services. In turn, construction required considerable labor.

At the same time, the influx of European immigrants to North America was at its peak. Ports from Montreal to Philadelphia processed people by the boatload, many of whom subsequently dispersed themselves by rail up and down the Atlantic seaboard and to the Midwest.

The City of Washington's demand for labor, especially during the 1860s and 70s, coincided with waves of Irish and German immigrants reaching American shores. African Americans, Italians, and various Eastern Europeans rounded out the city's population expansion through the 1800s. But among these groups, the Germans and the Irish cohabitated most easily at work, in residential neighborhoods, and particularly for Catholics, in church. Their children readily intermarried. The men quickly became the backbone of skilled trades of all description.

While certain professional strata passed through the nation's capital with the churn of political administrations, the German-Irish population became by strength of numbers a cornerstone of Washington's working class from the Civil War though the first half of the 1900s.

This was the milieu from which the orphaned Philip originated. A Catholic couple seeking to adopt a child in Washington, D.C. during the 1930s would probably pursue their quest through local Catholic institutions. Prevailing customs of racial and ethnic segregation would be observed by the institutions that cared for orphans. Similarly, a mother with an unwanted pregnancy was likely to seek assistance from the institutions of her own community.

If a preponderance of the city's Catholic population claimed German-Irish roots, then presumably its orphan population would be proportioned similarly. Lacking definitive proof to the contrary, it is likely that Philip Thomas Hughes descended from German-Irish heritage.

# CHAPTER 3

# Tom and Wilhelmina

Thomas and Wilhelmina Hughes adopted Philip no earlier than 1934. Newly arrived in Washington that year from Indiana, the Hugheses were Catholic in both spiritual and social contexts. Married only at the onset of middle age, the couple had no children of their own. Each having grown up with many siblings, they may have found that married life was incomplete without children. For Wilhelmina, motherhood was a sense of obligation rooted in her Catholic faith.

Nineteen-year-old Thomas Theobald Hughes crossed the Atlantic Ocean in 1903 with what was then the equivalent of $80 in his pocket. He left Scotland on October 2 on the Allan Line's *S.S. Sicilian*, a 430-foot, single-stack steamer that typically ran from Glasgow to Boston or Halifax, Nova Scotia. Tom disembarked at Quebec City, Canada on October 12. In very short order, he boarded a train bound for the United States, which he entered through St. Albans, Vermont. He reported to U.S. border officials that Springfield, Illinois was his intended destination.

Tom hailed from Chapelhall, a village in North Lanarkshire, just east of Glasgow. He was one of nine children born to Patrick Hughes, an Irish coal miner, and his Scottish wife Mary. Patrick, Mary, and their five youngest sons – all either current or soon-to-be coal miners – would emigrate to Illinois. Tom's 1903 solo crossing was effectively a reconnaissance for the rest, who followed him in 1905.

Date unknown. Allan Line's *S.S. Sicilian. Vintage postcard image.*

Knowledge of the coal mining industry was one of the few assets the Hughes family brought with them from Scotland. All were literate, but seemingly content with (or resigned to) the risks and rewards of their trade. By 1910, the family had settled at 2131 South 16th Street in Springfield, Sangamon County. Among the sites where they found work was the Klondike Mine at Springfield Junction.

Tom would quickly see professional opportunity in collective labor organization. It was in this capacity that he met and befriended John L. Lewis, an Iowa-born miner with an intense personality and ambition that, in 1920, got him elected president of the United Mine Workers of America. During the coming decades, Lewis would make headlines as the advocate of coal miners' interests.

Meanwhile, Tom Hughes was entrusted with the union's membership relations. At a height of five feet, six and one-half inches, Tom was not imposing; instead, his blue eyes and square jaw conveyed a calm, confident demeanor. Lewis sensed Tom's ability to connect with the average coal miner, thus making him an effective liaison with rank-and-file union members.

Tom's outreach in this capacity required extensive travel through coal country to organize miners and negotiate on their behalf. He paused in 1917 to become a naturalized citizen, possibly in response to the First World War then raging in Europe. Naturalization would release Tom from any obligations he might have had to Great Britain due to his Scottish heritage.

American citizenship would also boost Tom's credibility among the union's constituency. Similarly, he learned to rid his voice of the Scottish burr of his youth, adopting in its place the flat Midwestern accent of central Illinois.

May 1923. Springfield, Illinois. Passport application photo for Thomas Hughes (1884-1968). *www.familysearch.org.*

Through these years, Tom remained a bachelor, which rendered him free to travel without encumbrance. But by 1923, Tom needed a break from the series of boarding houses in which he found lodging throughout the Ohio River valley coal country. Closing in on age 39, he applied for a passport, indicating the intention to leave in June of that year for Scotland, England, Ireland, and France to "visit relatives and [for] pleasure." It may be that Tom, like so many other immigrants, returned to his homeland to fetch a spouse. What he sought most in a wife was someone to take care of him. If that was his goal, Tom returned to America empty-handed the following September.

Tom passed frequently through Indianapolis, where the Mine Workers' Union maintained its headquarters. It was in this city that he patronized a certain shoe repair shop managed by Wilhelmina Knue.

Wilhelmina's grandparents had come to Indiana from the Lower Saxony region of northwest Germany by way of Cincinnati, Ohio in the early 1800s. By the end of that century, Wilhelmina's parents, Frank and Mary, abandoned farming for the opportunities offered by urban living. While Wilhelmina and her siblings grew up in the small town of Aurora, Indiana, most of them eventually made their way to Indianapolis.

The Knue children were well-educated. George became a surgeon. Cyril became a priest, a vocation that led to his becoming the president of St. Joseph's College of Indiana, and later, a representative to the Vatican. Older brother John Francis also chose a religious vocation; as a pastor, he built a new church and school across the Ohio River in Kentucky. Louis, the entrepreneur, established shoe repair shops in Indianapolis, entrusting their daily management to his siblings Joe, Gesina, and Wilhelmina.

It is not easy to overstate the importance of the Catholic Church to the Knue family.

Wilhelmina was educated by Franciscan nuns at the Oldenburg Academy, a convent school in southeastern Indiana. The convent's curriculum included the classics, painting, music, and domestic science. After graduation, she was active in her church choir and played piano.

Tall and trim, Wilhelmina matched Tom Hughes in height. Like many of the Knue siblings, she had a square face with deep-set, piercing eyes that gave her a somewhat eagle-like countenance. Wilhelmina was an industrious, intelligent woman with business acumen and a knack for organization.

Tom asked Wilhelmina to be his bride. When they married in May 1928, Tom was 44 years old. Wilhelmina was age 38. Because their parents were all deceased by this time, the couple opted for a low-key ceremony. A wedding day photo shows Tom and Wilhelmina on the rain-soaked steps of a church rectory, accompanied by a handful of Wilhelmina's siblings.

The photo depicts John Francis as a tall, burly man in crisp, priestly clericals; he may have been the presider. The matron of honor was Wilhelmina's sister, Gesina. Cyril, the other brother-priest, joined them. Cognizant of her age, Wilhelmina eschewed a bridal gown for a straight-cut walking suit and a cloche bucket (the hat of choice for women in the 1920s). Tom wore a dark three-piece suit, probably the best selection from his office wardrobe.

Without Tom's boutonniere, Wilhelmina's corsage, and the Knue sisters' bouquets, there was nothing about their appearance to suggest that it was their wedding day.

May 1928. Indianapolis, Indiana. From left: Thomas Hughes (1884-1968), Wilhelmina Knue Hughes (1889-1969), Rev. Cyril F. Knue (1895-1943), Gesina Knue Kennedy (1882-1943), Rev. John Francis Knue (1879-1945). *Courtesy of the Hughes family.*

# CHAPTER 4

# Moving to Washington

The stock market crash of 1929 heralded not only the Great Depression, but also life-altering changes for Tom and Wilhelmina. They would leave Indianapolis for Washington, D.C., where the federal government was ramping up to become the primary force of economic recovery. Franklin Delano Roosevelt ascended to the White House in 1933 armed with radical plans for proactive government spending to jump-start the moribund economy.

Industry leaders made anxious by the worsening Depression could not help but notice the volume and variety of spending by Roosevelt's administration. If they were not there already, numerous trade associations, news agencies, and lobbyists of all description found it imperative to relocate to Washington, D.C. They did so in hopes of boosting their exposure to Congress, the White House, and the capital's burgeoning administrative agencies.

In Washington, federal payrolls alone more than doubled between March 1933 and 1940. It was during this era that many monolithic federal headquarters came into being. The massive Federal Triangle complex displaced the old Center Market and the rough-hewn area known as "Murder Bay," located directly south of Pennsylvania Avenue. The Departments of Interior, Commerce, Agriculture, as well as the current Supreme Court building were constructed or expanded during this time, as was a new congressional office building and an annex to the Library of Congress. But even this was not enough, as World War I-vintage offices of "temporary" construction were not only retained, but overhauled for a new generation of bureaucratic activity.

None of this growth was lost on the mine workers' lobbyist John L. Lewis. As a headquarters location, Indianapolis was central to the miners he served, but it was over a day's train ride from the nation's capital. And so, in July 1934 the United Mine Workers of America moved its operations and key staff to Washington, D.C.

John L. Lewis (1880-1969), president of the United Mine Workers of America from 1920 to 1960. *Sangamon Historical Society.*

The organization rented space for a couple of years in the Tower Building on K Street until purchasing the former University Club located at the southwest corner of McPherson Square. The UMWA staff quickly modified the interior of this handsome Italian Renaissance Revival structure to suit their needs, adding a sixth floor. They moved in by Christmas 1937.

Meanwhile, Lewis and his wife Myrta took up residence across the Potomac in Alexandria, Virginia. They purchased the stately Lee-Fendall mansion located on a half-acre lot at the corner of Washington and Oronoco Streets. Lewis's chauffeured car could deliver him to UMWA headquarters in under half an hour, if there was no back-up on the 14th Street Bridge.

The Hugheses rented a home, also in Alexandria. By this time, Tom was well established – and paid – as a union executive. He would be described today as a "senior vice president for member relations," or something similar. But at the time, Tom was shrewdly bestowed the unassuming title of "clerk." Lewis understood that his rank-and-file members struggling through the Great Depression would likely balk at paying dues to a trade union rife with pretentious executive titles. At the same time, the simple title would presumably make Tom more approachable in the course of his membership relations duties.

Tom brought home the paychecks, while Wilhelmina managed all their household dealings with thrift and efficacy, even laying out the clothes Tom wore each day. She keenly handled their finances, drawing from her family business acumen and the "domestic science" studies from her convent days. Almost as soon as the Hugheses were settled in their Alexandria apartment, they began thinking about scaling up to a house – and perhaps starting a family.

Tom and Wilhelmina's search for a permanent home in Washington, D.C. coincided with the city's unprecedented boom in new home construction. Driven ultimately by the growth of New Deal program staffing, the economic expansion of the nation's capital was the envy of most other cities. Speculators during the 1930s snapped up virtually all the remaining undeveloped land within the District of Columbia.

New construction, largely to the north of the downtown area, provided a variety of detached and multifamily structures. Almost all of it was densely packed. The most frequent design was the row house, cheap to build and thus offered at prices within reach of most government employees.

While Tom carried out his daily work at the UMWA headquarters, Wilhelmina made frequent excursions across the Potomac to scout real estate options in the city. A leisurely ride one day on Capital Transit's gently rolling No. 80 streetcar line took her almost four miles due north of Union Station to the terminus at 12th and Quincy Street in the city's northeast quadrant. She would soon decide that this area, Brookland, offered what she and Tom needed.

She discovered a charming new row house development there on 10th Street. The units were simple brick construction, each offering essentially the same floor plan. But unlike the monotonous frontal geometry typical of row houses, these had articulated facades. The pitch and orientation of gabled rooflines varied across these dwellings, as did window configurations. Fluted wood trim, especially around the doors, reflected Georgian architectural stylings inspired by antebellum Virginia mansions. Wilhelmina's unit of choice faced east, absorbing morning sunlight without obstruction. But make no mistake: these were practical dwellings, easy on the budget, yet removed from the hub-bub of downtown.

The Hugheses sought not only a house, but also a cultural affinity for the community where they would live. These were typical American aspirations at the time, when cities still consisted of ethnic enclaves. This tendency was only reinforced by the real estate industry's widespread use of covenants that barred the sale of homes to certain ethnic groups.

C. 1940. The functional heart of Brookland, 12th and Monroe Streets, Northeast Washington, D.C. *D.C. Public Library Washingtoniana collection.* © Washington Post.

As a result, the Brookland community that Wilhelmina discovered in 1934 was inhabited primarily families of Irish and German descent, with some Italians. Jews and African Americans were scattered throughout in lesser numbers, but these groups were often forced by custom to travel outside the neighborhood for shopping, schools, and personal services. What most households had in common, however, was a wage earner who worked downtown.

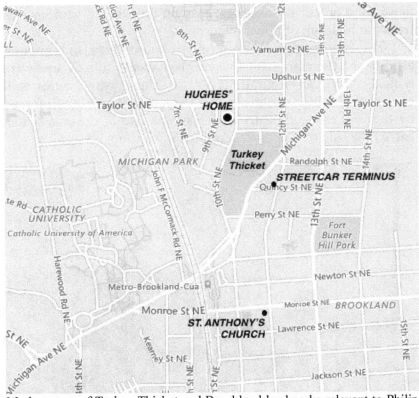

Modern map of Turkey Thicket and Brookland landmarks relevant to Philip Hughes. The street layout remains virtually unchanged from the 1930s. *Internet screen grab, subsequently annotated.*

Brookland's town center, if it could be called that, evolved around commercial establishments clustered at the intersection of

12th and Monroe Streets, which was made convenient by the streetcar line that rounded this corner. Here were Brookland's post office, the Sanitary and a couple of other grocers, Haske's Bakery, Doc Hall's drugstore, Moore's hardware store, the Hamilton Bank, Newton Theater, a few shoemakers, and other small-scale commerce. Cast-iron water troughs remained on the sidewalks, scattered throughout the village. Placed before the turn of the century, these troughs served the diminishing number of mules that teamsters still drove through the 1940s, delivering coal or blocks of ice.

St. Anthony of Padua, a Catholic Church, was also here in Brookland's center, a healthy eight-block walk from the Hugheses' new home. If they wanted, however, the Hugheses could hop on the streetcar at 12th and Quincy to cover much of that distance. A direct walk from their house to the streetcar terminus cut across a flat, grassy parcel that somehow escaped development.

That parcel, perhaps a dozen acres in total, was what remained of Turkey Thicket.

<<<>>>

"Turkey Thicket" was the name ascribed to a colonial land grant issued in 1733 by Charles, Lord Baltimore to a Scotsman named John Magruder. These 350 acres were located in what was then Maryland, which at that time was a proprietary colony in that it was owned by shareholders whose interests were managed by a royally-appointed governor.

Magruder, like most Maryland colonists, anticipated wealth derived from tobacco and slave labor. Turkey Thicket's harvest could be rolled in hogshead barrels to the wharves either in Bladensburg or Georgetown, both of which served ocean-going vessels.

Turkey Thicket, as well as the neighboring parcels named Cuckhold's Delight and Beall's Inclosure, would change hands and sub-divide over the years. The tobacco fields and cow pastures were first transformed by the encroachment of Fort Bunker Hill and related fortifications built by Union soldiers

21

during the Civil War. Not long after, in 1873, powerful railroad investors secured land to create B&O Railroad's Metropolitan Branch, which connected Washington, D.C. to the Ohio River valley. The railroad's right-of-way sliced across Turkey Thicket.

Late 1861. The tract known colloquially as "Turkey Thicket" hosted Union Army units preparing to enjoin battles in Virginia. At the time of this photo, the 31st Pennsylvania Infantry was encamped here. Each of the conical tents accommodated up to 16 soldiers. Newly-constructed Fort Bunker Hill appears on the horizon to the right. *Library of Congress.*

In 1886, the Archdiocese of Baltimore purchased a 66-acre parcel immediately west of the railroad to develop the Catholic University of America. During that same year, elderly landowner Jehiel Brooks died in Bellair, his mansion constructed on the former Beall's Inclosure patent. Once a bucolic plantation great house, Bellair was a scant 200 feet east of the newly constructed rail line, opposite Catholic University. Brooks's heirs quickly sold the land to speculators.

The next 50 years brought slow but steady development to the area as the University's presence prompted additional construction by a variety of religious orders and institutions. An early collection of Victorian frame houses with large yards gave way to a dense grid of row houses. Commercial infrastructure evolved in step with housing. This became the Brookland community, named in tribute to Jehiel Brooks.

# CHAPTER 5

# Adoption

For Tom and Wilhelmina, the move to Brookland was an exclamation point to their good fortunes. Income security that evaded so many others at that time was not a problem for the Hugheses, especially because they settled on a property that was well within reach of Tom's income. Tom's cocktail lunches with Capitol Hill staffers and industrialists brought a new and perhaps even glamorous phase to his career. One of Tom's executive perks was to have a car and driver dispatched for his door-to-door commute.

But despite the excitement of living in a new city, Wilhelmina sustained a gaping want for children. Resigned to the inevitable, she investigated opportunities for adoption.

The concept of adoption in 1934 contrasted sharply with what the Hugheses witnessed during their youth. The late 1800s and early 1900s saw the use of "orphan trains," organized by aid societies to transfer orphaned children – often dozens at a time – by rail from the industrial cities of the Northeast to various Midwestern towns.

This ostensibly charitable practice was the initiative of social reformers in response to the staggering number of homeless street urchins found in large East Coast cities. Advance notices through farmers' church assemblies drew prospective foster parents to railroad depots. There, the newly-arrived orphans were lined up for review and selection by farmers eager to obtain additional (cheap) labor. The benevolence offered by adoptive parents varied widely; some orphan train children were more fortunate than others.

Whatever the shortcomings of this approach, society at the time preferred it to leaving children to fend for themselves in the wretched streets and alleys of industrial cities. Having knowledge of the orphan trains, Tom and Wilhelmina were motivated to do better by providing a permanent, loving home to a deserving orphan.

Over many long conversations, the Hugheses formed their vision for a family. Wilhelmina wanted two sons, both to assume the *Hughes* surname. Tom did not share Wilhelmina's yearning for children. Nor did he oppose it. Rather, he accommodated her wishes, making it clear that the duties of parenting would be hers alone. Wilhelmina accepted this.

May 16, 1946. A view of the infant ward at St. Ann's Infant Asylum, Washington, D.C., taken more than a decade after Philip Thomas Hughes matriculated through the same facility. *D.C. Public Library Washingtoniana collection.* © Washington Post.

The Catholic Church would be their primary resource for adoption. Through St. Anthony's parish, Wilhelmina contacted St. Ann's Infant Asylum, a venerable Washington, D.C. institution staffed by the Sisters of Charity of St. Vincent de Paul. Leading this staff was the asylum's matriarch, Sister Rose.

St. Ann's main facility was located on Washington Circle in Foggy Bottom, at 2300 K Street. The oldest part of this red brick, three-story mansion dated back to 1820. It housed the British Legation to the United States prior to its conversion to the infant asylum during the Civil War. Just under 100 children were housed there, all under six years of age, along with a few indigent, unwed mothers.

When Wilhelmina first visited St. Ann's, Philip was about two years old. He was already capable of scampering about the asylum's playrooms and yard.

The asylum's interior was day-lit by long, narrow windows. A large room on the first floor featured the kitchen with rows of low tables lined with tiny chairs. Upstairs, wards for the infants featured rows of cribs constructed of metal frame tubing. Those infants not yet ready to walk spent much of their days in baby swings suspended above their cribs. Toddlers tended to gravitate to the sun parlor to employ a set of oilcloth rocking horses. Many children enjoyed an assortment of balls that they rolled or bounced around in the playrooms.

Outside, to the rear, was a rose garden planted decades earlier by a British consul general. Here, the children could amuse themselves with wagons, swings, and slides. Washington Circle was across the street, where a couple of nurses could occasionally roll out a batch of tots in a pull-cart. In this park, the children enjoyed fresh air and sunshine, perhaps the only resources available to the orphanage in abundance. They frolicked about the shaded green beneath the bronze equestrian statue of George Washington.

The asylum, plus the park, were Philip's universe.

Institutional staffing at St. Ann's ensured that Philip interacted with a variety of caregivers throughout the day. Some were nuns dressed in full religious habits. Supplementing them were nurses dressed in white uniforms. But in either case, these caregivers walked a fine line, being attentive to the children without becoming emotionally attached. Meanwhile, Philip's cohabitants of similar age did not interact so much as they all played independently in the same space.

Philip was accustomed – unconsciously, of course – to the scent of wood, horse-hair plaster, urine, and disinfectant all comingled within the asylum. Itinerant smells arose throughout the day, associated with meals or when he or one of his associates needed a diaper change. During the winter, acrid smells sometimes wafted from the relief valves of steam heating radiators distributed throughout the building. But every time he returned from the outdoors, these particular aromas instantly assured Philip that he was "home."

Another constant in the asylum was noise, to which he readily contributed. Like any tot, Philip's vocabulary was limited, but he could experiment as he pleased with the pitch and volume of his voice. The din within St. Ann's was largely unabated, except for nap times and at night.

Perhaps the most imposing constant was the rhythm of Philip's daily life, paced by meals, baths, naps and playtime. During his early, formative years, Philip would be nurtured not by a mother, but by a structured routine.

This was the little boy who caught Wilhelmina's eye. She picked him up. His response while being held in her arms was endearing. A chemistry was evident.

The choice was mutual.

He already responded to the name "Philip." The ensuing adoption legally recorded a new middle name, chosen as a nod to Tom.

And so this child became Philip Thomas Hughes.

<<<>>>

If adoption granted Philip the love and security of a family, it also meant removing him from everything that he knew up to that point. Few would argue that an institution struggling through the Great Depression would provide a child with a home better than one offered by adoptive parents.

Orphan asylums are almost always fiscally challenged. During the Depression, the ratio of children per staff might have been even more onerous. Resource constraints ensured that infants lacked the benefit of continuous engagement that an ever-present mother would provide. Add to this the rotation of caregivers caused by institutional staffing. Patchwork care and nurturing during the first year of an infant's life has critical consequences for the child's later capacities for judgement and social interaction. Even as adults, they may retain an inordinate tendency to act impulsively.

Decades later, the psychological community would formally recognize this phenomenon and label it *reactive attachment disorder*. Philip was born into circumstances that placed him squarely at risk of developing such a condition.

Good, bad, or otherwise, the vagaries of institutional care during his earliest months of life would indelibly shape Philip's personality. The Hugheses probably anticipated the adjustment issues posed by an adopted child, just as they pondered their own capacity to love and nurture a child not of their own bearing. In the end, they counted on the positives exceeding the negatives. Parental discipline inspired by tenets of faith would fill any gaps.

Whisked off to the house on 10th Street, young Philip's world was instantly reinvented. His routine – and indeed, his universe – were completely upended. He found himself in a new space, much smaller with completely different dimensions and sources of light. It smelled different. Gone was the cacophony of other babies lined up on either side of his crib. So too was the rotation of care givers, replaced now by one woman who fed him, bathed him, wiped his nose, and sang him to sleep.

Until this time, Philip had never learned – or needed – to address anyone as *Momma*, *Mother*, or *Mom*. This woman in his new environment demanded exactly that. As days became weeks,

Philip learned that *this* woman (and *only* this woman) was his provider, companion, and source of comfort.

In the meantime, the Catholic charity network identified a newborn baby boy in Philadelphia. This infant was born to a teenaged girl from a well-to-do Philadelphia Main Line community. The family had apparently made discreet arrangements for their daughter to bring her child to term and then put it up for adoption. The time of the infant's birth serendipitously coincided with the Hugheses' search. A healthy, newborn white male was all they were looking for.

Unlike Philip, this adoptee would be accepted sight unseen. A nurse bundled up the baby and took him on a two-hour train ride from Philadelphia to Washington, D.C., where he was transferred to the Hugheses through St. Ann's Asylum.

Born in 1934, this boy would be named Francis Joseph Hughes, or by nickname, *Frank,* just like Wilhelmina's father.

Wilhelmina intended to instill Catholic faith and traditions in her adopted sons. She quickly arranged a baptism for newborn Frank. In all likelihood, the staff at the infant asylum had already done so for Philip.

Ultimately, the adoption of Philip and Frank fulfilled not only Wilhelmina's maternal needs, but would serve her Catholic obligations as well.

# CHAPTER 6

# Growing Up

With three bedrooms, a basement, and about 1,350 total square feet, the Hugheses' home in Brookland was deceptively spacious. Philip and Frank would each have his own bedroom – a veritable luxury during the Depression and war years, when many Washington households included boarders.

The yard was modest. It had just enough space in front to accommodate Tom's penchant for flower gardening, and in the rear, a radial clothes line. The backyard was bounded by an alley, and across this were the rear exposures of two-story apartments that faced 9th Street. In front, just across the street and down one short block, the open expanse of Turkey Thicket became a communal, all-purpose playground for neighborhood kids.

Running a household was an arduous task for a family without an automobile, and the burden fell solely to Wilhelmina. At no time did the Hugheses employ a domestic helper. So while Tom worked downtown, most of Wilhelmina's day was filled with routine housekeeping and laundry chores.

She devoted a lot of time to grocery shopping, venturing four or five blocks on foot to the village markets on 12th Street, year in and year out, at the mercy of the weather, with two little boys in tow. She had to shop often because her purchases were limited to what she could drag home in the boys' little play wagon.

She certainly took advantage of diaper service and dry cleaning delivered to the door by Bergmann's Laundry. Similarly, a Thompson's Dairy milkman brought daily deliveries of fresh milk in glass bottles, deposited in a galvanized metal box on the doorstep.

Shopping for clothes, furniture, or other major items meant catching the streetcar downtown to 7th and F Streets Northwest. The selection of department stores included Woodward & Lothrop, Kann's, and Landsburgh's. Such excursions ate up the better part of the day, so the boys could count on getting a lunch counter hot dog at Peoples Drug Store or perhaps the Hot Shoppes.

Early 1940s. F Street, N.W., the shopping district of Washington, D.C. The nation's capital remained vibrant through the Great Depression and World War II. *Image from a historic trail street display.*

Tom was content to relax at home, leaving the vast majority of domestic chores to Wilhelmina. Perhaps this was consistent with the times, or just his nature. Or both. At the end of each day, he settled into his armchair for several hours to read a selection of newspapers.

As a father, Tom was largely disengaged from the boys. He tended his flowers and cut the grass. There were no fishing or camping excursions. Tom was not a story teller, so he shared few if any memories about his youth in Scotland. Years later, Frank could recall only one way that Tom connected with him and

Philip. Tom took the boys on an occasional stroll up Taylor Street to the overpass that spanned the B&O Railroad below. There, they could enjoy the mix of steam and diesel locomotives pulling passenger coaches and boxcars. Standing at the handrail directly overhead, the boys counted the hopper cars in the coal drags that were a mile or more long.

Like all the kids in Brookland, Philip and Frank took advantage of the long days of summer, which allowed ball games on Turkey Thicket to continue well after eight o'clock. As the daylight faded away, fireflies rose from the grass, issuing their blinking yellow lights in the night air. The fireflies' arrival meant it was time for children to come inside for the evening.

At home, with the windows open on summer nights, Philip and Frank fell asleep listening to the frequent rumbling of locomotives plying the B&O. Occasional whistle blasts were accompanied by the metallic ringing sound of train wheels flanging the rails.

As the boys grew, they were allowed to venture down on their own to the nearby commercial strip on 12th Street, if not to run shopping errands, then to catch a matinee at the Newton Theater. Mr. Moore, owner of the village hardware store, also opened up the Brookland Bowling Alleys just a couple blocks south of the Hugheses' home on 10th Street.

A large, wooden cabinet radio in the living room provided the entire family a connection to the outside world. The boys could lie on the floor to stare at the radio's grill, entranced by serial adventure stories like *Captain Midnight* or *Superman*. Sometimes they opted for comedy like *The Jack Benny Show* or *Fibber McGee and Molly*. As the 1930s drew to a close, the focus of news broadcasts increasingly switched from economic policy to ominous portents of war in Europe.

The Hugheses enjoyed an occasional Saturday excursion to Glen Echo, the fabulous amusement park located west of the city above the Potomac River. The park offered a roller coaster, a merry-go-round, and the Crystal Pool with its daredevil waterslide. But equally thrilling was the ride to the park on the tree-shaded Number 20 trolley line. The route skirted the upper banks of the Potomac, giving the passengers a breathtaking view of the rocky river below. Unlike the herky-jerky ride in city traffic, the streetcar journey to Glen Echo featured long, straight stretches with few stops. The motorman could delight the riders by opening up the throttle, approaching 50 miles per hour at times. In the era before air conditioning, the breeze flowing through the trolley's open windows was a reward in itself.

Excerpt of the 16th Census of the U.S. (1940), recording the Hughes family in Washington, D.C. The circled "X" means that Wilhelmina was the census taker's respondent. It shows that Tom was age 55, born in Scotland, and had eight years of education. Wilhelmina, age 50, born in Indiana, had four years of high school. Philip is described as age seven and born in Washington, D.C. The census lists Frank as age five and – erroneously and perhaps purposely – shows D.C. as his birthplace. *National Archives: 1940census.archives.gov.*

Starting in 1937, the Hugheses began making annual excursions to Rehoboth Beach, Delaware, on the Atlantic Coast. At the time, a trip to the beach from Washington, D.C. involved a ferry crossing of the Chesapeake Bay. Still without an automobile of their own, the Hugheses traveled by bus. The entire trip consumed the better part of a day. With its delightful ocean breezes, Rehoboth gave the Hugheses welcome relief from the stifling Washington, D.C. summers.

Rehoboth offered a boardwalk and a beach that stretched for miles in either direction. Philip and Frank enjoyed the beach, or at least the break it provided from the monotony of Brookland. Wilhelmina was indifferent to the sand and the ocean. She did, however, take note of Rehoboth's real estate, which included a collection of summer homes all within a couple blocks of the boardwalk.

Years of scrupulous saving allowed the Hugheses to accumulate an appreciable nest egg. Wilhelmina bought a cottage on Newcastle Street, giving the family a home base for their summer excursions. Through the 1940s, she continued buying additional cottages as income properties on the same street.

Vintage beach cottages on Newcastle Street, Rehoboth, Delaware. *Author's collection.*

As the Brookland community grew during the 1930s, so did St. Anthony's Parish. By 1938, the parish replaced its original 1896 frame chapel with a much larger edifice of wheat-colored brick. Reminiscent of a bank in its stoutness, the new church was tempered somewhat by Mediterranean design elements inspired by the Basilica of St. Francis of Assisi in central Italy. The church's grammar school was similarly appointed.

Philip Hughes was one of 900 children enrolled in the school, absorbing the Catholic catechism along with standard academics. His commitments to St. Anthony's required daily visits to the campus: Monday through Friday for school, confession on Saturday, and Mass on Sunday. Philip's commute from his home to the church traced along Turkey Thicket – back and forth, throughout all his grammar school years.

Catholic teaching obliges the faithful to attend Mass every Sunday. But for every Catholic who fully understands the theological tenets of the church, there are countless others who perceive catechetical direction as an obligation beyond reproach: They go through the motions because they are told to do so.

More to the point, Catholics frequently conform to family tradition. German and Irish grandparents, for example, could not surrender memories of the persecution suffered by ancestors back in the "old country." Spiritual dividing lines fostered an us-versus-them community outlook. Immigrants persevered by applying that clannishness to interactions at school, at work, and in social life.

The working-class German-Irish community in Brookland functioned like a tribe, bound as much (or perhaps more) by the momentum of ethnic allegiances rather than religious ideology. But while Catholics were predominant, they shared the neighborhood with a fair number of Protestants. Dividing lines among faith communities were generally innocuous, but nevertheless convenient to adolescents seeking to develop pecking orders among themselves. Confrontations rarely involved more than name-calling between groups walking to and from school. "Cat-licker" was one of the taunts that Philip Hughes might have encountered on his walk to school.

Tribal perseverance compelled many Catholics – if not most – to crowd into the pews for Mass each Sunday. In those days, the Roman Catholic Mass was conducted in Latin. While congregants could follow a missal with the appropriate translation, it was useless to small children whose restlessness so often spoiled the solemnity of the liturgy. But before they could even hope to understand the *meaning* of the Mass and its components, Philip, Frank and all the other children were expected to learn and practice the rote conduct of a congregant – when to stand, kneel, genuflect, and apply the sign of the cross. Some children found the experience excruciating; others found a way to tune out the proceedings and drift in their own thoughts.

The Catholic Church recognizes seven years as the "age of reason." At that age, the church considers children able to discern right from wrong. This is the criterion for receiving first communion, that is, to participate fully in the sacrament of the Mass for the first time. First communion is a cause for celebration by the child's family. Thanks to parish boundaries that encompassed almost 2,000 families, St. Anthony's matriculated dozens of first communicants each year.

The parish organized an annual May procession for a community-wide celebration for each year's crop of communicants. This involved coordination with the Metropolitan

Police Department, which barred traffic from the 1000 block of Monroe Street to accommodate a parade of children, the girls dressed in little white bridal dresses with lace, and boys in white shirts and black pants. A team of older boys led the procession, one bearing a crucifix and another with a lit censer dispensing incense. The parish's pastor, Reverend John J. Coady (who insisted on being addressed as "*Doctor* Coady"), brought up the rear of the procession, often accompanied by seminarians. Singing *Immaculate Mary*, the children paraded onto the church grounds, where an appointed girl would adorn a statue of the Virgin Mary with a wreath of flowers. Philip's turn to walk in the May procession came in 1940.

After Philip and Frank achieved their first communions, the Hugheses required both sons to be altar servers at St. Anthony's. The boys joined ranks with others, perhaps ten in total, each outfitted for the Mass in black, ankle-length cassocks covered by a white, smock-like surplice. Altar servers were assigned a myriad of tasks. Some boys were candle and cross bearers for the opening procession. Others held liturgical books from which the presider read; rang bells to announce consecration; and carried bread, wine, and collection offerings to the altar. But aside from delegating these practical tasks, the church was introducing boys to the elements of consecrated life. In other words, altar serving was a way to prepare boys for the priesthood.

The attack on Pearl Harbor in 1941 drew America into the Second World War. The pace of activity in the nation's capital redoubled on a wartime footing. Perhaps it was this change in the environment that inspired Wilhelmina to gather the boys together for a discussion one day. Their friends, she said, were bound to question why she and Tom were so much older than the other kids' parents.

Wilhelmina explained their adoption for the first time.

But that was not all. Wilhelmina announced that she expected both Philip and Frank to become priests. She wasn't asking them... she was telling them. Being accustomed to their mother's rigid guidance, neither boy doubted this directive.

A Catholic tradition encouraged families to direct their oldest sons – or the "firstfruits," as the Old Testament would refer to them – to enter the priesthood. Wilhelmina's family upheld the tradition when her brothers Cyril and John Francis answered the church's call. She held the same aspirations for not one, but both of her adopted sons.

Wilhelmina began steering the boys toward activities commensurate with religious vocation. Her approach to parenting was inspired by her convent education under the Franciscan nuns. She was a vigilant observer of the boys' every move, be it table manners, posture, or approach to household chores. She reprimanded them at her whim for doing anything she deemed inappropriate.

It was as if the boys were an extension of her will. Wilhelmina played piano, so she would have her sons do the same. Frank readily obliged her lessons, but Philip would have nothing to do with it.

Perhaps Wilhelmina's most curious initiative required Tom to construct a replica of an altar in the basement. He did this using a combination of spare furniture and some lumber from Mr. Moore's Brookland Hardware. Outfitted with the requisite cups, plates, and candlesticks, Philip and Frank were encouraged to play at being priests, conducting a "pretend" Mass. The boys were already committed to attending the St. Anthony's campus six or seven days per week. But even that was not enough to satisfy Wilhelmina.

By revealing to the boys their adoption, Wilhelmina admitted, in effect: *I'm not who I always said I am*. Philip and Frank were not truly sons, but were enablers of her agenda.

The boys began to contemplate rebellion... but how?

Philip and Frank came to realize that Wilhelmina's revelations undermined their identities. Neither boy could articulate his sense of betrayal and entrapment, yet their ensuing struggle with Wilhelmina would bond the boys in a way that blood did not.

And so began the Battle of Turkey Thicket.

# CHAPTER 7

# The Changing City

Philip Hughes reached his 13th birthday just as World War II ended. He was athletically built and naturally strong, coming to Wilhelmina's aid whenever she had trouble opening a jar or turning the knob on a stuck door. On the playground, Philip got a reputation for being a tough kid. Anyone who dared to scrap with him would not make the same mistake twice.

Frank was not similarly gifted, being small for his age. While he was not yet as capable as Philip in navigating the rough-and-tumble culture of adolescent school boys, Frank nonetheless cohabitated well with Philip, who protected his little brother as occasions required. With a two-year age difference between them, Philip and Frank each formed his own circle of friends from the surrounding neighborhood.

When he completed elementary school, Philip proceeded to secondary school downtown at St. Mary's. His daily commute on public transit provided a taste of independence as well as a vantage point for witnessing a changing city.

The nation's capital continued to absorb an influx of people from all over the U.S. during the war years. Newcomers to Washington brought with them regional affinities, tolerances, and expectations to what was still a culturally "southern" city.

Change was afoot. The long-standing practice of racial segregation in employment, services, and schools in Washington, D.C. became a flashpoint of protest and legal conflict. This began in earnest during the war, notably when picketers protested Capital Transit's policy of hiring only white operators for its buses and streetcars.

Similar challenges continued after the war. Jackie Robinson broke the color barrier of baseball's major league in 1947. The next year, President Harry Truman issued an executive order that called for the desegregation of U.S. armed forces. The Supreme Court struck down the enforceability of real estate covenants that restricted the sale of housing to buyers of prescribed ethnicities. Newspaper headlines described frequent picketers who challenged the segregation of shopping and dining facilities. Protests at Washington, D.C.'s segregated, city-owned swimming pools sometimes turned violent. Given that America had just expended exorbitant wealth and blood to defeat fascism, courts simply could not uphold the legal foundations of societal segregation.

Nineteen forty-eight was the year that newly-installed Archbishop Patrick O'Boyle ordered the desegregation of Catholic schools in the archdiocese of Washington, D.C. This would immediately include Gonzaga and St. John's, the Catholic boys' local high schools of choice. The archbishop shrewdly asked the press to not publicize this decision. Instead, the news traveled by word-of-mouth within the Catholic community as O'Boyle made the rounds with church councils and school administrators. At some parishes, resistance strained the Archbishop's persuasive skills to the limit. He sometimes resorted to scripture to convince skeptics of the righteousness of this initiative.

Like many people, the Hugheses were afraid of the unknown consequences of desegregation. As a young man, Tom saw first-hand the fury of mob violence fueled by racial animosity in the two-day riots that ripped through Springfield, Illinois in August 1908. Tom was fearfully impressed by both the mob's ferocity as well as the utter inability of police and militia to contain the violence. Wilhelmina's family had witnessed much the same in the Cincinnati riots of 1884. Most people in Washington were at least apprehensive about desegregation. Tom and Wilhelmina harbored some deep concerns for their sons' welfare in a mixed-race school setting.

Public schools remained segregated at the time, but that was of no matter to the Hugheses because these were not *Catholic* schools. Searching for other options, Wilhelmina consulted trusted advisors in the church community. Among the suggestions offered to her was to send the boys to Canada, presumably populated by the "right" kind of people, thus giving her peace of mind about her sons' scholastic environment.

She identified a solution in the form of St. Jerome's, a Catholic boys' boarding school in Kitchener, Ontario, which appealed to Wilhelmina on a couple of dimensions. For one, German Lutherans and Mennonites figured prominently among early settlers in the Kitchener area. Additionally, St. Jerome's administered both a high school and a college – presenting possibilities for the boys to receive future seminarian training.

In preparing to leave for Canada at the end of summer 1948, Philip and Frank, ages 16 and 14, respectively, anticipated their first travel of any consequence aside from their summer trips to Rehoboth Beach. For the first time, the two boys would travel without parents.

Wilhelmina had Philip recite the itinerary she prepared. The train trip to Kitchener involved multiple segments via western Maryland and Pennsylvania. It included the massive Buffalo Central Terminal in New York, and then crossed the International Bridge over the Niagara River and into Canada. Wilhelmina dutifully saw the boys on their way from Union Station.

A train ride through the heart of the northeastern United States in 1948 provided alternating vistas of farms and factories, wilderness and cities. From the window of his speeding coach, Philip saw massive steel works, quarries and kilns, refineries and granary silos. His journey passed countless rail yards with team tracks where workmen operated a variety of trucks, cranes, and tractors. The passenger coaches often passed between long unit trains of coal hoppers. The train's entry or departure from a city usually involved a river crossing on a trestle, with dramatic skyline views. In rural areas, long stretches were punctuated by the occasional farmhouse or barn. Cows, horses, and other livestock dotted the landscape. When his eyes tired of tracking the panoply of sites, Philip relaxed his focus to allow the scenery to flow by in a blur.

For a boy whose links to the outside world were previously limited to radio broadcasts and the occasional movie theater newsreel, the train ride to Kitchener must have been nothing less than intoxicating.

Arrangements were made with a prefect from St. Jerome's to escort the Hughes brothers from the Kitchener train station to the school. The high school building was a massive block; four stories of bulk rose from its rectangular footprint. For whatever consolation it gave Philip and Frank, the building somewhat resembled the public McKinley High School in Washington, D.C., as its design elements included a red brick façade, heavy concrete borders, and prominent ionic columns.

2007. Kitchener, Ontario. The former St. Jerome's College, now part of Sir Wilfred Laurier University. *Parks Canada website.*

The boys settled into the 1948-49 academic year, learning how to function and socialize in a boarding school setting. St. Jerome's boasted about 70 boys per grade, some commuting locally, with boarders from all over North America and beyond – including Philip and Frank – making up the balance.

St. Jerome's provided both social and academic structure, with classes usually conducted by prefects robed in clericals. Dormitory living was supervised by room captains. As a Canadian institution, St. Jerome's was not tremendously different from its American counterparts. Activities included a glee club, a photography lab, and the occasional chaperoned dance, which allowed the boys to meet students from the affiliated St. Mary's school for girls. Canadian flavor was evident in athletics. The Americans, or "Yanks," as they were good-naturedly called, were introduced to rugby and curling in addition to basketball and track and field.

Removed for the first time from the "tribe" in Brookland, the boys were struck by the cultural catharsis presented at St. Jerome's. Philip now found himself bunking in a communal setting that may have revived his distant memories of the orphanage.

Meeting kids from different places, each with a unique background and life story, Philip could not help but ponder his own origins. Who were his real mother and father, and what happened to them? The experience at St. Jerome's would have ignited an aching need to know who he really was. And did the new setting – or more specifically, the change itself – provide respite from his dissonance with Wilhelmina's expectations?

The Battle of Turkey Thicket escalated, if only in the confines of Philip Hughes's thoughts.

# CHAPTER 8

# Runaway

As Philip and Frank Hughes approached the end of the 1949 school year, their dread of returning home to be cloistered by their mother was rekindled. With some disgruntlement, the boys bid farewell to their friends at St. Jerome's that June and made the reverse journey back to Washington, D.C.

Travel tickets had been arranged in advance, simplifying Philip's role to that of Frank's chaperone as they negotiated the rail connections. Tom and Wilhelmina met them at Washington's Union Station, escorting the boys the rest of the way home on a familiar grey-over-green Capital Transit streetcar.

Wilhelmina must have known that her sons weren't happy with her expectations. Neither boy longed to resume "playing priest" in the dark, unfinished basement of their home.

What could she do about it? Summer was, of course, an opportunity for the Hugheses to return to their cottage in Rehoboth. Some family time at the beach would allow them to talk through things in a relaxed setting. Perhaps then, she thought, the boys would warm up to her wishes.

The bus trip to Rehoboth began with an easterly ascent from downtown on New York Avenue, past Bladensburg and onto Route 50 across the Maryland countryside. Within a couple of hours, the road met the Chesapeake Bay at Sandy Point, just above Annapolis.

The state of Maryland owned the Chesapeake Bay Ferry Systems, which consisted of a fleet of double-ended ferries. Each vessel was named for a former Maryland governor, hence labels like *Gov. Harry W. Nice* or *Gov. Herbert R. O'Conor* stenciled on their bridges. Perhaps 200-260 feet long, each ferry carried up to 75 vehicles.

C. 1949. The *Gov. Emerson C. Harrington II*, one of the Chesapeake Bay ferries linking Maryland's eastern shore with roads to Washington, D.C. *Talbot (Maryland) Historical Society.*

Vehicles would queue up for the next scheduled ferry to shuttle them to Matapeake on the eastern shore. From there, the road ran in long, straight stretches across Delaware's corn fields and pine forests before reaching the terminal at Rehoboth Beach.

Rehoboth was a quiet settlement in 1949. Sun and sand, water and wind – these were the visitor's rewards.

A few frame hotels and a rudimentary collection of shops lined town's beach-front boardwalk. Summer cottages surrounded this core. It was a place where outsiders came to relax as opposed to busying themselves. During the summer, the town swelled with visitors from Washington, Baltimore, and Philadelphia. A year-round population of carpenters, fishermen, shopkeepers, and their families rounded out the community.

Tom and Wilhelmina brought their sedentary habits with them to Rehoboth. Wilhelmina brewed coffee every morning which the two shared while perusing the daily newspapers.

Wilhelmina also kept busy with managing her portfolio of rental properties.

Meanwhile, Philip and Frank had all of Rehoboth at their disposal. They could toss a football with other kids on the beach or frolic about in the surf. Hiking north along the waterline took them to Cape Henlopen, where they could explore a couple of concrete coast-watching towers that loomed up from the dunes. These structures had been abandoned a few years earlier after the Army was certain that Delaware was safe from Nazi invasion.

C. 1946. Rehoboth Beach, Delaware. The *S.S. Thomas Tracy*, a shipwreck and, briefly, a tourist attraction. *https://www.reddit.com*

At a point just opposite the center of the boardwalk, the remains of two ships were lodged in the beach. The wood-sparred *Merrimac* ran aground in 1918. Its keel entrapped the collier *SS Thomas Tracy* when it just so happened to run aground at the same spot in 1944. Both ships had been largely salvaged down to the waterline, with the remnants combining to form a landmark that beckoned to be explored.

Despite the change of scenery that Rehoboth provided, it offered only so much to do. Stalking about the cottage with a flyswatter had limited appeal. Just steps away at the end of Newcastle Street, the boardwalk was a venue where the boys could peruse the penny arcades or pick up an ice-cold soda pop.

If Philip furtively spied girls on the boardwalk, then it was certain that they noticed him in return.

It is also from Rehoboth's boardwalk that the morning sun appears to rise directly from the ocean. When summer storm clouds roll across the sky, they cast an inky darkness on the water below; yet ahead of the front, the skies and ocean waves glisten together beneath the unabated sun, oblivious to the approaching weather. The vista was unlike any seen in Washington, D.C. With this unobstructed view of the horizon, Philip could detect the curvature of the earth. It was here that he could watch freighters from Philadelphia exiting the Delaware Bay on their way out to sea – approaching, meeting, then crossing the horizon as they dwindled completely from sight.

<<<>>>

The Hugheses' cottage was not only close to the beach, it was also two short blocks from St. Edmond's Catholic Church. Diligent about their religious obligations, they made this little beach-side chapel a surrogate for worshiping at St. Anthony's.

Since the order of Catholic Mass was universal, the boys knew instantly what to expect from their weekly hour of worship. But here in Rehoboth, as back home, Wilhelmina infused expectations of piousness into every aspect of the boys' daily lives. Nothing less could be expected of her priests-in-waiting. Her way was the only way, no matter where they were.

In a sense, Wilhelmina *was* the church.

If religion was not the cause of estrangement between Wilhelmina and the boys, it was certainly a catalyst. A truly devout Catholic lifestyle nurtures the spirit of Christ from within so that it can be shared with others. The tenets of Catholic faith are embodied in sacraments of initiation, healing, and service. The sacraments are rites and channels through which the grace and spirit of God manifests among a community of faithful.

In this way, faith is transformed into practice, fostering a tangible spirit that becomes its own reward. The daily, conscious practice of sacraments form a *discipline that serves faith*. By way of analogy, a brick by itself is of little use. An assembly of bricks, however, creates a durable structure. In much the same way, the Holy Spirit is the mortar that bonds individual Christians who practice their faith together as a community. Parents, priests, and other catechists play a crucial role in mentoring faith in catechumen – the individuals being groomed for full communion with the church.

Mentoring works fine if the mentor is truly committed to the student's growth and understanding. However, the relationship is vulnerable to mentors with a predilection for control who are willing to manipulate the innocent in ways that satisfy the mentor's agenda. When that happens, the dynamic is reversed so that *faith serves discipline* elicited for the mentor's satisfaction.

While this was probably not Wilhelmina's conscious approach, it was still the outcome. There was a fuzzy line between her responsibilities to faith versus the family traditions rooted in her Teutonic heritage.

While both boys chafed at their mother's domineering ways, Frank's alienation edged toward combativeness. He developed an uncomfortable dissonance: Any natural dependence on "Mom" clashed with a growing dislike, not only for the agenda given to him, but also for the woman who imposed it.

Defiance of Wilhelmina was not an option.

At the same time, Philip became increasingly restless. Far from knowing what he wanted from his own life, he was only convinced about what he didn't. He was still the orphan for whom it was natural to fall asleep each night without a mother's embrace. Learning of his adoption must have sparked a groundswell of existential angst.

*Wilhelmina was not who she always said she was.* Philip's concepts of "home" and "family" were no longer immutable.

In the end, rather than preparing him for Wilhelmina's vision, traveling to Canada and enrolling in St. Jerome's gave Philip a hint of life beyond the confines of Brookland. He had been irrevocably exposed to a variety of people, each with a unique history and expectations about life. The very act of travel – to escape Wilhelmina's yoke – was itself a reward.

So there, at Rehoboth Beach during the summer of 1949, Philip decided to run away from home.

If Philip Hughes ever displayed the impulsive tendencies so often ascribed to institutional orphans, this was the time. There wasn't much premeditation. He correctly anticipated Frank's willingness to collaborate. Philip figured they would just go back to the house in Washington, pack up a few things, and buy a couple of train tickets.

The thought of a train ride – a ride going anywhere at all – became irresistible. So, after a mid-summer day's breakfast, Philip and Frank stepped out of Wilhelmina's beach cottage, letting the screen door slam behind them.

A journey had begun.

It would be easy, they thought. They had enough pocket change for bus fare back to D.C. While Wilhelmina assumed her sons were headed to the boardwalk, Philip and Frank casually strolled down Rehoboth Avenue, the main drag, away from the beach. The combination train and bus terminal was at the west end of town, just across the canal. The buses ran like clockwork.

Clambering warily aboard a coach bound for Washington, D.C., the boys began to feel the thrill of accomplishment only as the bus got underway. They perceived their point-of-no-return as it squeezed onto the ferry at Matapeake. When the ferry engine throttled up, Philip and Frank looked at each other with excited anticipation, knowing that the Bay crossing distanced them farther from their mother – and all that she imposed.

The return trip from the beach always seemed shorter for some reason, and this time was no exception. By mid-afternoon, Philip and Frank were back in Washington. Their home on 10th Street was locked, of course. But that was no matter. They coursed through the alley to access the rear entrance. Stepping down to the below-ground basement door, Philip jimmied the lock. They dodged the play altar and dashed upstairs to get what they would need. Some clothes. And some money.

Philip retrieved a wad of bills he had stashed away. Frank was momentarily perplexed. Was this left-over allowance from their travel to Canada? Philip seemed to have it all figured out. Anyway, it was time to go.

Philip and Frank Hughes, brothers and accomplices by fate, stole out of the house on 10th Street. Starting out on foot, they crossed the street toward Turkey Thicket and points unknown.

Where were the boys? They had been gone since morning and failed to return for lunch or dinner. By nightfall, Tom and Wilhelmina's concern was serious.

They found the Rehoboth Beach Police Department to be of little use. Chief John Zeallor had 11 men at his disposal, a secretary, a second-hand typewriter, and one patrol car, which was distinguished by insignia on its side doors and on the trunk. Rehoboth police were accustomed to issuing traffic violations or collaring the occasional drunk. A total of six arrests per year was normal. Foot patrol officers were briefed about the Hugheses' sons, but could turn up nothing over the next several days.

The Hugheses ran out of vacation time. Should they stay or go home? Distraught and bewildered, Tom and Wilhelmina made the return bus trip back to D.C., where they reported their missing sons to the Metropolitan Police Department.

They were forced to settle into an excruciating series of days, knowing only that their sons had vanished into thin air.

# CHAPTER 9

# Chicago

Among the boarders at St. Jerome's was a kid from the little town of Deshler, Ohio. Philip had befriended him in the dorm as they swapped stories about their train rides to Kitchener. As it turns out, Deshler featured a railroad junction where the B&O Railroad passed on its runs between Washington and Chicago. Philip must have gotten the kid's address, and at best, a standing invitation to "drop by sometime."

And now, solely at Philip's discretion, that time had come.

1963. Grand Lobby of Washington's Union Station. This scene is largely unchanged from Philip Hughes's visit in 1949. *National Archives.*

It was already late in the day when Philip and Frank strolled into Washington's cavernous Union Station. The boys knew the drill now: they marched between the lobby's sturdy mahogany benches to a row of ticket windows, each marked overhead with signs indicating "RAILROAD and PULLMAN TICKETS." They approached an agent who, like all the others, stood on a raised platform behind an array of steel-barred windows.

Philip asked the agent about their options for reaching Deshler. The B&O had four daily trains from Washington to Chicago, but only two – the Chicago Express and the Columbian – stopped at Deshler, Ohio. In either case, it was a 12-hour ride.

Consisting of Pullman sleepers, the Express departed at 2:15 p.m. The all-coach Columbian, departing at 4:40 p.m., cost less. Given the boys' late arrival at Union Station, the Columbian was the best option, and just in time, too. With a ticket in one hand and a travel bag in the other, the boys approached a gateman who pointed to the track where the Columbian was boarding.

In 1949, highways and airlines were just beginning to erode the railroad's domination of cross-country passenger travel. But in the meantime, rail was still the best option for many travel connections.

The B&O was nowhere near giving up its business. The Columbian had just been upgraded in April with a new set of eight streamlined coaches, including a Strato-dome observation car – impressive to behold on the platform, but of limited value to riders on the overnight west-bound leg. At least the Columbian offered the novel amenity of air conditioning.

Within five minutes of its departure from Union Station, the Columbian ran under the Taylor Street overpass – the same vantage point from which Tom Hughes and his adopted sons once watched trains passing to and from the nation's capital.

Philip and Frank would certainly have been hungry as they began their trip, seeking the dining car for a hamburger and a Coke before settling into a reclining coach seat for the long, westward ride. By dusk, the Columbian entered West Virginia and ventured deeper into the Allegheny Mountains, crawling steadily for over 100 miles through the rocky cuts that lined the B&O's Sand Patch Grade. The boys were asleep before the train reached Connellsville, Pennsylvania at 10:00 p.m.

The eastern horizon was still dark when the boys disembarked from the Columbian at Deshler just after 4:00 the next morning. Having enough sense to wait for daylight, Philip and Frank crashed on the station's benches for a few more hours.

<<<>>>

The town of Deshler had little to offer the visiting tourist in 1949. Located in northwestern Ohio about 50 miles south of Toledo, Deshler's most significant feature was the junction where the B&O's east-west rails crossed those of the north-south Dayton & Michigan line. During the war, lots of servicemen passed through the train station to switch lines, but traffic had dropped off dramatically since.

Philip led Frank to his buddy's address.

*Uh, what a surprise! Come on in, boys. Stay with us? Well, sure.* Hospitality was extended that day, and the next. And the next.

It was still summer, so there were no school obligations. Philip, Frank, and their classmate had the run of the town, including a recreation spot with a pool table that Philip put to good use. The boys made it back each evening in time for dinner.

*So... who exactly are these boys, son?*

The sheriff got a phone call. The stand-off was short but decisive. Into the pool hall came the sheriff, whose solution was to order Philip and Frank on their way. Out of town. Problem solved.

Having gone this far on the B&O, Philip figured that Chicago had much more to offer and was only another three hours away. So the boys hopped a train that pulled them through northern Indiana and across the Illinois state line, where the railroad skirted Lake Michigan before snaking through the dense maze of Chicago's industrial south side. The ride finally terminated at the B&O's Grand Central Station on Harrison Street, just west of the lake front.

Accommodations were immediately an issue. The YMCA appeared to be the best bet, and it was only a few blocks away. So Philip and Frank once again set off on foot, immediately struck by the vertical scale of Chicago's streetscape. They were accustomed to buildings in Washington that were purposely regulated to not exceed the height of the Washington Monument. The largest building they had ever seen at home was the Main Post Office on Pennsylvania Avenue – the equivalent of 12 stories. The Chicago Board of Trade had 44 levels.

The boys' destination was a tremendous landmark in its own right, made unmistakable by the large, rooftop neon sign reading "YMCA Hotel." Located just south of the Loop at 9th and Wabash, the YMCA boasted 2,000 rooms arrayed on 19 floors.

C. 1940. Chicago YMCA, 826 S. Wabash Avenue. *Vintage postcard.*

Encountering the desk clerk, Philip regarded his options and selected a lower-story room on the building's rear side. It had two beds, a dresser, a table and chair and not much else. A wash basin may have been installed in the room; shared toilet and bath facilities were located down the hall. A single window faced west. Looking down, the boys could see the roofs of passenger trains traversing the Chicago Transit Authority's elevated rail above Holden Court.

A choice of two cafeterias offered a mix of counter and table seating. The prices were reasonable, but Philip's wad of bills was running low. He already paid some rent in advance. His next priority was to get a job, which he quickly accomplished.

How exactly did Philip and Frank spend their days in Chicago? It was still summer, so the appearance of truancy was for now a non-issue. How much money could a 16-year-old make by washing dishes or pumping gas?

C. 1950. Chicago. Having run away from home with his brother Philip during the summer of 1949, 15-year-old Frank Hughes explored the sights, sounds, and odors of Chicago's Skid Row. *Tumblr.com.*

Philip's employment left Frank to his own devices, allowing him to roam about the immediate neighborhood. He wandered through Chicago's Loop, the traditional heart of the city's business district, its streets topped by steel girders that supported overhead passenger trains. Heading west from the Loop, Frank discovered Madison Street, lined with the bars and flophouses of Chicago's Skid Row. Touring this area involved stepping over and around drunks sprawled on the sidewalk. Back at the YMCA, Frank found a piano at his disposal in the East Room. But what else was there to engage his attention? There were no other kids and no open space like Turkey Thicket.

The excitement of travel and discovery could only last so long. They spent perhaps a week in Chicago, or maybe 10 days. Philip was the mastermind of the escape, but had no vision for an end-game. Frank was no help. Both boys had to become frustrated at some point.

The YMCA manager broke the impasse. Responsible for the integrity of the hotel, the manager kept an eye on all the characters lodging at the "Y." He certainly noticed the two teenage boys becoming increasingly grimy with each passing day. Neither boy gave a thought to tending his laundry. The manager decided to intercede, cornering the Hughes brothers one day in the lobby. *What gives, fellas?*

Exhausted by their new circumstances, the boys fessed up. The manager realized that he had runaways on his hands. Philip provided the number for a Washington, D.C. phone exchange: HO-2676. Wilhelmina answered the call.

The Hugheses were relieved of their worst fears. Wilhelmina notified the D.C. police of this breakthrough. But a resolution was not yet at hand.

The remedy involved the Metropolitan Police Department's dispatch of a female officer by train to Chicago; she would escort the boys back to Washington. After an awkward 12-hour ride, the boys were met at Union Station at 8:30 in the morning by a humiliated and furious Wilhelmina Hughes.

By running away from home, Philip made a point, expressing disgruntlement he could not put into words. But now Wilhelmina had her own point to make. She had the authorities take Philip and Frank away immediately to reform school.

# CHAPTER 10

# Reform School

As August 1949 drew to a close, Philip Hughes turned 17. No festivities marked this milestone. Rather than packing up for a second year at St. Jerome's, Philip and his brother Frank joined the inmates of Washington, D.C.'s Industrial Home School.

Located just north of Georgetown, tucked between Wisconsin and Massachusetts Avenues, the school's campus was adjacent to the U.S. Naval Observatory. The school was established in 1875 by absorbing the pre-existing Poor House of Georgetown, providing a home of last resort for truants, delinquents, orphans, and children transitioning between foster homes.

The title "Industrial Home School" was a compound malapropism: while the campus included a 1902-vintage school building, the curriculum offered next to nothing in the way of industrial arts. The institution's emphasis on temporary enrollment undermined the sense of "home." As for academic offerings, the school was a far cry from its D.C. public counterparts, much less the top-tier Catholic schools like Gonzaga or the new DeMatha High in near-by Hyattsville.

The Industrial Home School was by this time an obsolete firetrap, overdue for demolition. It had no fire alarm or sprinkler system. There were fire escapes from the upper levels, but the windows that would have provided egress were barricaded by heavy wire mesh screens. Without these barriers, boys would sneak out at night for clandestine visits to the liquor store across Wisconsin Avenue.

Rudimentary dormitory accommodations included lines of steel-tube bedframes and wooden cubby-hole shelves for storing any belongings. Sleeping quarters were upstairs. Unpartitioned toilets were in the basement, where the floors collected water from leaking pipes. The institution's scant resources ensured that culinary and janitorial services were executed with indifference. Philip must have found the setting vaguely familiar.

C. 1946. Industrial Home School for Boys, 2400 Wisconsin Avenue, N.W., Washington, D.C. *Library of Congress.*

The Industrial Home School was chartered for the service of white children. African-Americans were pointedly excluded, yet the institution accepted humanity of every other description, including Native Americans and a fair number of Filipinos. Regardless of their ethnicities, these children emerged from a variety of hard circumstances, and too many of them developed aggressive or anti-social tendencies.

Philip Hughes, one of the tough kids from the Brookland tribe, could handle himself in reform school. His demeanor alone could discourage the would-be antagonist, but if it came to fisticuffs, Philip had the skill and power to prevail. The adjustment was not so easy for Frank. Still small for his age, he encountered repeated bullying, but Philip capably interceded on his behalf.

To what condition, and by what measure, would Philip and Frank be "reformed?" As always, the choices were up to Wilhelmina. Perhaps she wanted nothing more than to have punishment meted out. After all, scripture promises that suffering refines the soul. Maybe she thought the boys would emerge from this experience with greater appreciation for the life and aspirations that she provided for them... or so she hoped.

<<<>>>

September yielded to October. At some point, Philip realized that he was eligible to enlist in the armed services at the age of 17, if given parental authorization. It may have been brought to his attention by another kid, or even by an administrator. A recruiter may have visited the Industrial Home School.

What vocation for a tough kid could be better than... the *United States Army?*

Philip saw his share of war movies at Brookland's Newton Theater. Handsome film actors demonstrated time and again how well-trained American soldiers with superior weapons prevailed on the battlefields of Europe and on scattered Pacific islands.

With World War II behind them, boys in the U.S. Army could look forward to an exciting overseas enlistment, touring foreign lands in a crisp uniform, enjoying lodging, meals, and on top of that, a paycheck – all courtesy of Uncle Sam.

Surrendering again to impulse, Philip Hughes decided to enlist in the United States Army. Wilhelmina signed for him.

There was an Army recruiting center in a somewhat seedy section of downtown at 403 10th Street, N.W., just above Pennsylvania Avenue. The many itinerant military men of Washington, D.C. frequented this strip with its bars and tattoo parlors.

In the recruiting office, some cursory screening was involved. The sergeant gave Philip a short written test and had him sign a letter of intent. These were the first items entered into a personnel file. Philip was also responsible for obtaining a letter from a law enforcement authority stating that he was in no way a fugitive of the law or had past or pending violations registered against him.

### HERE'S WHAT THE NEW ARMY OFFERS YOU

Before you choose any career, compare it with a future in the Regular U. S. Army. Never before has the Army offered such tremendous opportunities for a real career to the alert, ambitious young men of America.

On the one hand you have the chance to serve your country while learning a new trade or skill—to further your education in important fields. And on the other hand there are the financial advantages, the job security, the retirement benefits, the chances for rapid promotion, the free medical and dental care that are yours in the Army.

A career in the U. S. Army is an opportunity that just can't be beat. And it's a lifetime opportunity! Get the full details now at your nearest U. S. Army and U. S. Air Force Recruiting Office.

**PEACE IS AMERICA'S MOST IMPORTANT BUSINESS**

THE NEW ARMY AND AIR FORCE OFFER...
* WIDEST CHOICE OF CAREER JOBS
* BEST OPPORTUNITY FOR ADVANCEMENT
* UNUSUAL RETIREMENT BENEFITS

**US ARMY and U.S AIR FORCE**
RECRUITING SERVICE

November 24, 1948. One year before Philip Hughes enlisted, the U.S. Army Recruiting Center in Washington D.C. ran this advertisement (excerpt shown here) in *The Washington Evening Star. D.C. Public Library Washingtoniana Collection.*

58

The sergeant then explained the enlistment process and described some options for billets where he might be assigned. The Army maintained a large presence in western Europe, but America's deteriorating relations with the Russians were of growing concern. A tense, 12-month stand-off with the Soviets had only recently been resolved, only because the U.S. and allied air forces maintained an airlift to sustain civilians barricaded in West Berlin. If there were to be a war again, this seemed to be the most likely place.

Another option involved the U.S. Army's occupation of the Japanese home islands. Despite putting up a ferocious fight during the war, the people of Japan were anxious to eke out a living by coexisting with U.S. occupation troops. A wide range of services and entertainment were affordable to even the lowest ranking American soldiers stationed in Japan.

Philip was intrigued, if not by the options offered by the Army, then by the opportunity to quit reform school and travel once again.

By enlisting in the Army in November 1949, Philip satisfied a coincidence of needs. The Army gained another individual to maintain the manpower required for its overseas commitments. Wilhelmina may have perceived military discipline as an antidote for her son's insolent behavior. For Philip, the Army provided a way out of Brookland and the confines of Wilhelmina's control.

The worst that could happen was that there would be another war. But how likely was that? America had atomic bombs now. Many policy makers believed that foot soldiers would not be required in future conflicts. Their role, if any, would be reduced to constabulary duties.

Army enlistments were achieved on a rolling basis; there was hardly any wait. A couple of signatures and a handshake sealed the deal. Philip had a few days to report to the induction center at Camp Meade, a stop on the Pennsylvania Railroad halfway to Baltimore. He returned to the Industrial Home School to pack up his belongings.

Stunned to learn of his brother's enlistment, Frank would become immediately preoccupied with navigating reform school on his own.

# CHAPTER 11

# Basic Training

Within days of his visit to the recruiting office, Philip Hughes made his way to Maryland's Camp Meade for induction and his prelude to basic training. The main activities were physical examinations and competency testing.

A shuttle bus drove him and a handful of other young men from the Odenton train station to the camp gates. Alighting from the bus, the men were welcomed by a non-com (non-commissioned officer) whose first order of business was to teach the men how to line themselves up.

Next came a physical exam, conducted in a barracks where the men stripped naked and stood in line, shoulder to shoulder. Vital statistics such as height, weight, heart rate, and temperature were all recorded. A team of physicians and orderlies then examined the eyes, ears, nose, teeth, throat – and yes, every other orifice – for signs of disease or illness. Perhaps the most dreaded part was the "short arm inspection," which was the Army's vernacular for examining the penis for evidence of venereal disease.

Uniforms would not be issued until basic training. After the men redressed in their civilian clothes, a formal oath of enlistment was administered. Each recruit raised his right hand, and with prompting, recited an oath in which they swore to defend their country and the Constitution – with their lives, if need be.

Having accomplished this, they were in the Army.

Then it was on to an office where each man was assigned a unique, 10-digit serial number for identification purposes. Philip was assigned this one:

# RA13339858

The serial number conveyed several variables of information. "RA" indicated Regular Army, in that the bearer enlisted of his own volition; draftees were assigned a "US" prefix, while commissioned officers were designated with an "O." The third and fourth characters indicated the region of the U.S. from which the bearer came. The digits "13" represented Pennsylvania, Maryland, Virginia, and the District of Columbia. The balance of the characters was specific to the individual.

Enlisted men were assigned the rank of "recruit," a position that paid $70 per month in 1949.

The recruits proceeded to a classroom for receiving the Armed Forces Qualification Test, or AFQT, which sought to determine each recruit's aptitudes and level of intelligence by posing a battery of 100 questions. The test covered vocabulary, math, spatial relations, and mechanical ability. Results supposedly indicated the recruit's best fit, or "military occupational specialty."

Philip's MOS was indicated by "4745," the code for "automatic rifleman."

Philip received travel vouchers for Fort Knox, Kentucky, a vast complex where recruit training was but one of the many different activities conducted. Arriving with other recruits at the main gate, Philip was bussed through a maze of two-story, cream-colored frame buildings. His bus weaved around a fair number of olive-drab jeeps, staff cars, and two-and-a-half ton trucks. Landmarks on the base included the headquarters, a hospital, various chapels, and a post exchange (essentially a convenience store). Here and there were tanks and artillery pieces immobilized as lawn memorials. Surrounding all of this were parade and drill fields, a firing range, and – unique to Fort Knox – the U.S. Bullion Depository offset some distance from the rest of the base.

The bus finally unloaded its passengers in a large parking lot. This being the Army, the recruits very quickly learned that their first line of instruction came from non-coms who loudly bellowed anything they had to say.

The first day of basic training involved a series of processing steps. For Philip and his new colleagues, this meant hurrying ("double-timing") from one destination to the next, only to wait for the next administrator. One of their initial stops involved the services of a barber who trimmed everyone's hair down to the scalp. There was another physical, this time to get inoculations. The smallpox vaccination made some men woozy, while the typhoid shot began to ache hours later. The Army prescribed 20 minutes of push-ups as the "cure" for this.

Administrative tasks included the optional ratification of a life insurance policy at a premium of $6.15 per month, accruing to a beneficiary of the recruit's choice. Clothing issue was another step: everyone was measured for and received five sets of undershirts, briefs, and pairs of socks. They also received a single field jacket, khaki dungarees, a leather shaving kit, an overseas cap, a belt, and two pairs of boots to be worn on alternate days.

Added to this were the necessary elements of a "class A" or dress uniform: two button-down shirts, a neck tie, two pairs of uniform pants, a pair of dress shoes, a garrison cap, and a short-waisted "Ike" jacket. All of this was to be stuffed in a barracks bag, which the bearer could sling over his shoulder.

The men queued up to have their clothing stenciled to facilitate its redistribution after weekly laundry. Per convention, Philip's items were stenciled "H9858," representing his last initial followed by the last four digits of his serial number. At some point, the men were dispatched to a mess hall for lunch – lining up yet again to collect a one-piece compartmented tray on which the cooks would ladle out the day's culinary fare.

Once they were outfitted, the recruits were directed to a parade ground where they were lined up into formations and assigned a platoon identity for the duration of their training. One of those first-day exercises was to teach the men how to "fall in," that is, line up properly and stand at attention. Similarly, they had to learn how to undo their formation upon the order to "fall out." The recruits were introduced to the basic commands and responses needed to march in formation. Another task was to get each man squared away in his new living quarters.

C. 1941. Standard stateside Army barracks structure, a design replicated at dozens of bases across the U.S. Built to house troops training for World War II, the same structures later served troops destined for Korea and Vietnam. *U.S. Army.*

Like so many other bases at the time, Fort Knox had barracks space to spare, a legacy of World War II manpower requirements. These wooden, two-story structures were replicated in countless rows. Each had a dedicated, coal-fired heating plant but no air conditioning. Double-deck bunks were located on both floors, while the first floor hosted a latrine outfitted with six to eight sinks, a similar number of shower heads, and a half-dozen toilets, none of which included privacy partitions. Each man's personal sleeping accommodations included a three-inch thick mattress over a spring bed frame. Personal item storage was accomplished with a foot locker and an open shelf/armoire structure made of rough-cut lumber. The men were assigned their spaces alphabetically.

Before they would ever sleep in this accommodation, the men would fall out to collect bedding. They were then taught how the Army expected them to make up a bed. If the folding and tucking were done properly, one could bounce a quarter dropped on the center of the bed – the more bounces the better.

C. 1950. Interior view of basic training barracks, Fort Lawton, Washington. Philip Hughes's accommodations would have been very similar. *Photo by Joseph N. Roberts, courtesy of www.rocketroberts.com.*

After evening chow, the men had some free time in the barracks to get acquainted. Once again, Philip Hughes found himself in a communal living environment, meeting people unlike anyone he knew from Brookland.

Recruits at Fort Knox came from almost every state east of the Mississippi River. Virtually all were volunteers under the age of 21. Some, like Philip, were as young as 17. Many boys, but certainly not all, came from modest circumstances made even more tenuous by the Great Depression. Among Philip's barracks mates were boys who knew deprivation and hunger. Some grew up having to walk barefoot to school. But as a whole, this was a generation that learned to work hard without complaint or question. Their expectations of government were respectful, shaped largely by the New Deal. During World War II, their families pulled together with the rest of their communities to endure emergency rationing while juggling time and resources for a common cause. When the war was over, they saw their fathers and brothers welcomed home with great fanfare, followed by their access to education, housing, and business start-up benefits conferred by the G.I. Bill. Army recruits in 1949 expected more of the same from their enlistments.

Exhausted by the demands of their first day in the Army, most boys were relieved when the Charge of Quarters (CQ) turned the lights out at 10:00 p.m.

Just before dawn, the CQ returned to flick on the lights. *Rise and shine or you will be doing double-time!*

Rushing to dress and make up their beds, the men fell out of the barracks to line up for roll call. The platoon sergeant could, at his discretion, chew out the men if their pace was not to his liking. When that happened, the men would return to the barracks to await a renewed order to fall in. This exercise was often repeated ad nauseam at each barracks until the recruits reacted with breakneck speed. After the successful fall in, each platoon sergeant in turn barked, "All present and accounted for!"

These weeks of basic training were designed and conducted to convert civilians into soldiers. Recruits were "reprogrammed," both physically and psychologically. Harsh and demanding exercises displaced the recruits' natural self-interests and individuality with the sensibilities needed to function as part of a team, with fidelity to each other through extremes of duress.

A typical morning task for recruits was "police call," which was a grounds sanitation exercise. The men lined up abreast outside the barracks and walked straight in unison, each man stooping to pick up cigarette butts, bottle caps, or any other detritus found in their path.

The days were filled with more drill formation familiarization and calisthenics. These included push-ups, pull-ups, sit-ups, squat jumps, and a 200-yard run. Interspersed among physical activities was a sequence of classroom lectures. This included an introduction to the articles of war. Recruits sat through training films about the history and culture of the U.S. Army, as well as admonitions about their presumptive communist foes. Other films discussed military courtesy and personal hygiene in the field.

The real challenge was to avoid falling asleep in the classroom.

The recruits also took turns fulfilling kitchen patrol duty. Aside from peeling potatoes, KP involved the care and handling of kitchen utensils and appliances, using soap and a copious amount of very hot water. All of these activities were subject to unannounced interruption by inspecting officers who would demand immediate redress for any infractions they might detect.

About three weeks into the curriculum, each recruit was issued an M1 rifle. The .30 caliber M1 was introduced to the Army in 1936 and remained the standard infantryman's weapon throughout World War II and the decade that followed. Like all the other recruits, Philip was expected to memorize the serial number of the rifle issued to him.

The M1, with its smooth walnut stock and hand grips, became part of the equipment in his care. Philip learned how to disassemble and clean the weapon. Ammunition was issued only as needed for field exercises. In field training, he learned how to fire the M1 from standing, sitting, kneeling, and prone positions.

While the country boys usually had some familiarity with rifles, this was the first opportunity for Philip and most other city boys to handle one. He was certainly surprised by the power of this weapon. When he first fired it from a standing position, the recoil drove him backwards a step or two. It was not unusual for a recruit to get a bruised shoulder early in the training sequence, courtesy of the M1 rifle. Over the coming weeks, Philip and his colleagues honed their marksmanship on a firing range where targets were fixed at a variety of distances from 100 to 500 yards.

Basic training imposed field exercises intended to build stamina and endurance. Exercises included off-road marches and cross-country hikes. Sometimes the hikes were conducted when the men were fully outfitted with gear, including a 25-pound field pack, rifle, ammunition, bayonet, entrenching tool (shovel), first-aid pack, and a waterproof sheet which, if paired with the one issued to another soldier, formed a tent.

Near the end of most marches at Fort Knox came the pinnacle of challenges: Agony Hill. Each man in his own way prepared himself for Agony Hill's punishing ascent. An ambulance and a number of trucks followed the men on this march. The recruits were told that anyone could fall out at any time and opt for a ride, but doing so would commit that person to repeating eight weeks of basic training.

Philip and his platoon marked their progress with Saturday inspections. Preparation began each Friday night as the recruits set to work straightening up the barracks interior, polishing their boots, and cleaning rifles. On Saturday morning, the recruits stood at attention, each at the foot of his bunk as the company's commanding officer inspected each in turn.

The recruits turned out for inspection in their class A uniforms, which in 1950 was assembled around the "Ike jacket," a design inspired by a British World War II battle topcoat. Added to the U.S. Army's wardrobe at the suggestion of General Dwight D. Eisenhower, the Ike jacket was so named because the General was so often photographed wearing the same.

Worn over a shirt and tie, the short-waisted Ike jacket was tailored snug to the torso. It featured generously-cut sleeves with insignia sewn on both shoulders. Its broad lapel converged over the chest, revealing only a couple inches of the necktie below the knot. A pair of bellowed breast pockets provided both function and visual balance. Pleated khaki slacks and spit-polished low quarter shoes rounded out the class A uniform.

Topping off all of this was the post-war soldier's headwear of choice: the wedge-shaped, fabric garrison cap. Reminiscent of a child's folded newspaper boat, the garrison cap was often worn tilted a bit to the side, if only for the jauntiness of doing so. It was easily folded and tucked under the belt.

C. 1950. Fort Riley, Kansas. A platoon of U.S. Army recruits at the end of their 14-week basic training. The Ike jackets and garrison caps were typical of the era's Class A uniform. *www.koreanwar-educator.org.*

Immediately following their barracks inspection, the recruits lined up outside with rifles in hand for the *order arms* inspection – a drill almost as old as the invention of the rifle itself. The men stood at attention, each with the butt of his rifle on the ground with the barrel leaning against his right leg. With crisp, robotic movements, an inspecting officer approached from the right, wheeling sharply to his left to face the first recruit.

Under the officer's watchful eye, the recruit then assumed *port arms* by hoisting the rifle up to chest height between him and the inspecting officer. He then opened the bolt of the rifle to visually ascertain that the weapon was unloaded. He then repositioned the rifle to the order arms position. The inspection then repeated for each recruit in sequence.

As ceremonial as it was functional, the arms inspection exercise instilled pride in the recruits, individually and as a unit.

When Philip Hughes enlisted in November 1949, the U.S. Army was already functioning in the budget year of 1950. Fiscal austerity prevailed under Secretary of Defense Louis Johnson per the overall direction of the Truman Administration. A desire to stimulate post-war employment and prosperity ensured that resources for the military were drastically reduced.

Having released millions of World War II-era servicemen to civilian society, the military's deflated staffing was complicated by a rapid churn of enlistments. In 1946, the basic training curriculum was reduced from 14 to just eight weeks. The average quality of recruit declined, compared to wartime inductions. Also, the Army had enormous stockpiles of equipment left over from 1941-45 manufacture, which effectively brought the development of new weapons and hardware to a standstill.

Army leaders by 1949 were particularly disturbed by their deteriorating personnel situation. Far too many billets were being staffed with raw enlistees; an inordinate effort had to be devoted to remedial training. Despite the austerity measures, the Army managed to restore the length of basic training to 14 weeks, beginning in March 1949.

Philip Hughes was among one of the first cohorts to experience this expanded post-war training format. His curriculum included elements that were missing from the eight-week syllabus, such as night-time maneuvering and familiarization with a wider variety of weaponry. The time devoted to physical conditioning doubled; field exercises, tripled.

Philip's basic training sequence was punctuated by the Christmas holiday of 1949. The Army was unique among the branches of the U.S. military in pausing its training calendar to allow soldiers to return home for a Christmas break of approximately ten days. Recruits who did so traveled at their own expense. The base did not completely shut down; there were always some men who simply stayed on throughout the break, pursuing a collection of make-work chores to pass the time. Officers living on base with their families would sometimes invite a recruit or two to join them for Christmas dinner.

Did Philip go home? Or more to the point, would Wilhelmina welcome him at home? Even if he used the Army to take a hiatus from Catholic obligations, it's very possible that Christmas 1949 was one of the loneliest days of Philip's life.

Washington, D.C. was unseasonably warm in January 1950, with hardly a trace of snow. Still, on January 12, Secretary of State Dean Acheson donned his trademark homberg as he strolled into the National Press Club at the corner of 14th and F Streets, NW. Acheson held a press conference intended to clarify the Truman Administration's policy goals in the far east given the impending capitulation of Chiang Kai-Shek's Nationalist Chinese government to Mao's communist forces.

Acheson described a frontier outlining the territory which the United States intended to defend against communist aggression. This territory included U.S. possessions and protectorates such as Alaska, the Philippines, and occupied Japan. The defense of the rest, Acheson stated, would ultimately rely on the "commitments of the entire civilized world under the Charter of the United Nations."

In the years since, much has been written about the explicit exclusion of South Korea from Acheson's frontier. Did communist leadership interpret this message as U.S. disinterest in Korea? In effect, Acheson's speech, delivered just as Philip Hughes resumed his military training after the Christmas break, may have inadvertently lit the fuse that six months later began the Korean War.

Expanded by the Christmas exodus, Philip's basic training concluded at the end of March 1950. Following a last, formal inspection on Fort Knox's parade ground, he and his fellow recruits matriculated at the rank of private.

One of the first activities of any newly-minted private was to have his photo portrait taken in his dress uniform. Philip was no exception. He sent the prints home to his mother.

Each man was then eligible for three weeks of home leave before continuing to his assigned billet. Philip received orders to join the U.S. Army's occupation forces in Japan, with departure immediately following his home leave. He got in contact with Wilhelmina.

Through the change of seasons, the love-hate relationship between Philip and his mother tilted toward the positive, for reasons known only to the two of them. In April 1950, Philip returned to Washington, D.C. and his home opposite Turkey Thicket.

March or April 1950. Private Philip T. Hughes (1932-1950). *D.C. Public Library Washingtoniana Collection.*

# CHAPTER 12

# Goodbye, Brookland

Thanks to basic training, Philip Hughes became an intrinsically different person. The Army fed its recruits all the protein and carbohydrates they could eat. A rich diet of meat, beans, and potatoes, plus rigorous calisthenics, could dramatically transform a 17-year-old boy. Philip came home to Washington bigger in stature and more poised in bearing compared to the boy who ran away from Rehoboth Beach the previous summer. Shaving was now part of his morning routine. Tom and Wilhelmina had to restructure their estimations of their adopted son.

Home leave provided Philip an opportunity to rediscover some creature comforts that he used to take for granted. Topping the list was the luxury of extended morning sleep in a quiet room with a comfortable bed. Home cooking was a plus; his appetite amazed his parents.

But for these few short weeks, Philip was again expected to attend Mass. This especially included Easter Sunday, which fell on April 9. Wilhelmina washed and ironed Philip's dress uniform so he could wear it to church. The uniform was chosen not out of pretentiousness, but of practicality; he could no longer fit in clothes he wore prior to his Army induction. The parishioners at St. Anthony's marveled over the boy they had not seen since the previous summer.

Frank's situation had not improved. Still at odds with Wilhelmina, he remained across town in the Industrial Home School. Philip set out one Saturday to pay a call on his brother. His crosstown journey was resplendent with the landmarks of his life.

The first part was on foot, of course, across Turkey Thicket to the Brookland streetcar loop at 12th and Quincy. From there, the No. 80 rolled by St. Anthony's church before skidding down Michigan Avenue past Catholic University to North Capitol Street. It was then a straight shot to Union Station and Capitol Hill.

The route then turned sharply west to follow G Street, cutting right through the downtown shopping district before continuing on Pennsylvania Avenue, passing the Treasury Department. Next was the White House, vacant and shrouded by scaffolds at the time due to extensive renovations; Harry and Bess Truman enjoyed temporary lodging in the Blair House, just across the avenue.

After crossing 18th Street, Philip made one more transfer, this time to a No. 30 car bound for Friendship Heights. As the ride continued through Foggy Bottom, the streetcar rounded Washington Circle and passed the site of the now-demolished mansion that once housed St. Ann's Infant Asylum.

The No. 30 inched along M Street through Georgetown, turning the corner onto Wisconsin Avenue, where it began a steady northward climb. Finally, at Calvert Street, Philip hopped off the streetcar right at the edge of the Industrial Home School Campus. This visit marked the last time that Frank ever saw his brother.

As April passed, Philip grew restless and looked forward to his travels to Japan. But before he left, the boredom of Turkey Thicket was broken for a day.

It was Wednesday, April 19. A fire broke out just down 10th Street at the Brookland Bowling Alleys. Philip couldn't have missed it: the blaze mobilized 34 engines, four trucks, plus assorted rescue and ambulance squads. Nine firefighters were hospitalized due to smoke inhalation caused by the combustion of wax on the alleys' floors. Even though the interior was almost a complete loss, the structure's load-bearing walls remained intact. In time, the building would be reconstituted, but as an electric supply store.

Like the bowling alley, the social fabric of Brookland was on the cusp of rebuilding from the inside out. Desegregation and "white flight" were not the only forces involved. By 1950, Brookland's housing stock was becoming worn and obsolete. The old row houses lacked the wiring and piping needed to support air conditioners, washing machines, clothes dryers, and other conveniences that were becoming readily available. Many homes lacked accommodations for one automobile, much less two. With good roads expanding into Maryland and Virginia, it was easier to simply build a new home with modern appointments than it was to upgrade older structures. The availability of larger yards was also an attraction.

For the most part, it was the families with children that quit Brookland, while others would stay to become part of the new fabric. No longer narrowly defined as an enclave for the German-Irish Catholic tribe, Brookland – like Philip Hughes – was just beginning to forge a new identity in 1950.

Tom and Wilhelmina had additional reasons to consider relocation. Now age 66, Tom's career at the Mine Workers' Union was winding down. The Rehoboth Beach cottage beckoned as a year-round home, especially as Wilhelmina had purchased more investment properties there.

As April drew to a close, Philip packed his duffle bag for the long trip across country to the west coast. He opted for the Greyhound bus, which would provide an intimate, road-bound view of America's mountains, plains, cities, towns, and people.

On the morning of his departure, Philip dressed in his class A uniform. He posed with Wilhelmina in front of his childhood home for a snapshot. The photo shows them both with big smiles. Frank would ponder this image for decades to come. He suspected that Philip, despite his apparent discomfiture with Wilhelmina's expectations, was the favored son.

<<<>>>

Frank Hughes was perplexed by his brother's departure for the Army, wondering would become of the camaraderie and reassurance that Philip provided. He had little time to grieve.

After Philip's departure, the reform school's predators were now unfettered. Inevitably, a couple of humiliating altercations ensued. Frank made an alliance with a Filipino kid who showed him how to fight. The Industrial Home School provided plenty of opportunities to practice. Frank eventually became acclimated to reform school living.

As a matter of due diligence, the school's directors kept notes on all the boys. Frank might have been gruff, but not incorrigible; in fact, he showed flashes of great academic potential.

A call was placed to the Hugheses. *Frank does not belong in a reform school.*

By the fall of 1950, Frank would be back home in Brookland, forging a tenuous peace with Wilhelmina. Tom remained aloof. Not yet certain of the best academic path for Frank, they enrolled him in a public high school.

# CHAPTER 13

# Pacific Crossing

Philip's travel orders took him to a west coast port. This was probably Fort Lawton, near Bremerton, Washington, where he would be billeted for a number of days while waiting for a Military Sea Transport Service vessel to set sail.

Like so much military hardware at the time, MSTS ships were of World War II vintage. In 1950, these ships crisscrossed the Pacific with civilian crews. The typical ship's manifest for a crossing to Japan could count upwards of 500 soldiers. Dependents, personal possessions, and other cargo added to this number, although dependents' accommodations were separate from the troops.

The boarding process could take all day. After the mooring lines were thrown free of the deck, a tug boat would nudge the ship away from the pier.

Many of the men stayed topside to watch the proceedings as the ship became oriented in the shipping channel. A ship leaving Bremerton passed through the Strait of Juan De Fuca, at which point it was effectively out to sea. The passengers then settled in for an almost three-week voyage.

The ship's internal space was flexible in that the same compartments could be configured for either cargo or berths for troops. Bunks were canvas laced taut to a steel frame. Frames were four or five to a vertical stack. Soldiers suspended their duffle bags from the racks, lining the corridor with what appeared to be punching bags.

The northern route from Bremerton hugged the coast of British Columbia, bound for an intermediate fueling stop at Adak Island before curving around the globe to approach Japan from the northeast.

There wasn't much to do except eat, sleep, and play cards. Philip challenged many of his colleagues to arm wrestling matches; once in a while he might have gotten some real competition. A movie screening was available most days, while a modest book collection served as the ship's library. Most of these ships had a mimeograph machine, on which a clerk produced purple-inked newsletters each day for the passengers' edification.

1942. USS Tennant. Philip Hughes's 1950 trans-Pacific crossing was achieved on a World War II-vintage transport with accommodations very similar to this. *U.S. Army.*

Weather on the North Pacific is volatile. On calm days, only the dull throbbing of the engines would remind passengers that they were on a ship. At night, passengers would be mesmerized by an ocean surface alight with green and white phosphorescence. Rough seas were another matter, when winds and wave swells conspired to make a rough ride. From a porthole, one could look out and up one moment and see nothing but a wall of water; the next moment placed the ship on top of a crest, so that the same porthole showed only sky. Using stairwells became an adventure as the ship listed with the rolls of the sea.

When rough seas prevailed, passengers could both hear and feel the ship shudder when its propellers popped free of the water. The center of the ship was the fulcrum from which it pitched and yawed. The bow and the stern moved most in response to ocean turbulence. From a comfort perspective, passengers would prefer a bunk or station at the center of the ship, where irregular motion was minimized.

Seasickness was a miserable consequence of the ocean voyage. Like all other troops, Philip took his meals standing up in the mess hall. Food was plentiful, but many men had trouble keeping it down. Accordingly, the mess halls were prepared with drums of 55-gallon capacity lashed to the bulkheads. The smell of vomit blended with the aroma of diesel exhaust throughout the ship. If the seas were less punishing, seasick men could go topside and hang over the handrail to "feed the fish."

Passengers began to spot seagulls drafting alongside the ship, a sign that they were no more than a day or two from land. Accordingly, Philip's transport finally queued up to enter Tokyo Bay and, ultimately, the journey's end at the port of Yokohama, a critical seaport for U.S. military supplies inbound to Japan.

Offloading allowed dependents to disembark first, followed by their cargo. Troops lined up in *ad hoc* platoons for descending the gangplank and subsequent boarding on train coaches adjacent to the pier. Their next stop, not far from Yokohama, would be Camp Drake, an Army replacement depot – or "repo depot" – where soldiers would receive individual assignments to one of several division-level installations scattered across Japan.

# CHAPTER 14

# Japan

Japanese civilization in 1950 was literally rising from ashes. Few of its major cities were untouched by the last, viciously contested stages of World War II.

As the war in the pacific progressed, America and its allies expended an increasing number of lives to conquer Japanese-held territories. American forces closing in on Japan found enemy resistance becoming increasingly tenacious. War planners shuddered to think of the lives required to conquer Japan's home islands and achieve ultimate victory.

The chosen alternative was to leverage American airpower. Simply put, the policy was to bomb Japan into submission. Because so many Japanese structures were built chiefly of wood and paper, incendiary bombs were the weapon of choice for destruction. Flames consumed buildings and lives; yet many more lives succumbed to asphyxiation as the massive fires voided the atmosphere of oxygen. The Japanese (or at least their leadership) vowed to fight to the death in lieu of surrender. Anticipating an invasion of their country, Japanese women and children began training for hand-to-hand combat using bamboo spears.

More astonishing than the war's mad destruction – climaxed by the release of two atomic bombs – was the remarkable transition to peace. After Japan's surrender in 1945, neither vengeance nor resistance took root as America and its allies first occupied Japan, then sought to rebuild the nation's economy and society according to western principles. Reconstruction called for interim leadership: A Supreme Commander for Allied Powers that occupied Japan beginning with its surrender in August 1945. This task was bestowed upon the same person who led U.S.

forces to victory in the Pacific: five-star General of the Army Douglas MacArthur.

America began pouring its soldiers into Japan in 1945 within days of the armistice. General MacArthur established an office in the former Dai-ichi Life Insurance Company building in Tokyo. MacArthur and a staff of several hundred combined military and civilian administrators were tasked with Japan's reconstruction. The priority of the occupying armies – overwhelmingly American in its composition – was to disarm and demobilize the remaining Japanese military infrastructure. This was accomplished with astonishing speed thanks to the cooperation of Japan's defeated army and its citizenry as a whole, of whom about 30 percent were homeless.

Equally important was the dismantling of industrial infrastructure that supported Japan's war-making capabilities, funded in part by a thriving trade in Manchurian narcotics.

The occupation agenda then evolved into one of maintaining order while the Japanese people rebuilt a market economy and democratic political structure under direct and watchful American influence. Through both civilian and military cadre, the U.S. provided technical assistance to replace and modernize Japanese industry, agriculture, education, and healthcare infrastructures. In addition, the allied occupation provided a bulwark against any expansionist goals harbored by the Soviets.

While the British Commonwealth contributed up to 40,000 troops to the Japanese occupation, the U.S. forces numbered no fewer than 100,000. War veterans mustered out of the service as quickly as they could, forcing the Army to replenish its ranks throughout the late 1940s with very young recruits – usually under 24 years of age, with many, like Philip, only in their teens. By the end of 1949, over half the Army's ranks were under the age of 21.

Fortunately, there was no longer a war to be fought. Occupation troops filled their days with training, calisthenics, and a variety of intramural sports leagues to maintain some semblance of competitive spirit. The United States Armed Forces Institute organized a catalog of self-study courses including both high school and college credits. Soldiers like Philip who had not completed their secondary education could use their off-duty time to enroll in a selection of classes.

By most measures, the troops of the U.S. occupation forces in Japan were not the equivalent of battle-hardened World War II veterans. Nor were they trained to be. The American military's post-war preparedness was increasingly predicated on its monopoly of atomic weapons.

Whereas American soldiers in World War II trained and deployed together as units, young post-war recruits filtered in and out of Army billets as individual replacements. The wartime draft secured a good number of competent men that the Army would not have otherwise obtained. In contrast, post-war recruits brought with them an average of only two years of high school education.

Some boys were troublemakers, while others had to be coaxed into the service by promises of vocational training for clerical tasks, cooking, facilities maintenance, machine operating, and other skills that men could leverage later in civilian life. In turn, a training curriculum geared to the demands of occupation duty did little to foster the spirit and competence needed by a truly effective fighting force.

As Philip Hughes stepped foot in Japan in May 1950, he then belonged to the Eighth U.S. Army, the entity ultimately responsible for carrying out U.S. occupation duties in Japan. Headquartered in Yokohama, the Eighth Army consisted of four divisions, these being arranged from north to south as follows: the 7th Infantry in Sapporo, which was closest to Soviet territory; the 1st Cavalry, with responsibility for Tokyo and the port of Yokohama; the 25th Infantry in Osaka, and the 24th Infantry Division on the southernmost island of Kyushu.

By virtue of its location, the 24th Division was effectively at the end of the supply line in a theater that, for the time being, ranked near the bottom of the U.S. military's overseas commitments. This is where Philip was assigned from the Camp Drake replacement depot.

His assignment was further refined to the 34th Infantry Regiment, one of three regiments forming the 24th Division. Philip's next order of business was to secure transport to the 34th Regiment's headquarters at Camp Mower in Sasebo, located in Kyushu some 600 miles west-southwest of Yokohama.

Accompanied by dozens of other new arrivals, Philip's travel to Sasebo involved the use of wooden rail coaches that somehow survived the wartime bombing of major cities. Railroads and stations were among the first infrastructure to be restored after World War II, as these were critical to the movement of both military and civilian supplies. It was around these stations, so heavily trafficked by occupation soldiers, that a Japanese retail industry was largely reborn. Bars, cafés, inns, and mom-and-pop shops selling crafted trinkets and clothing provided Philip's first impressions of Japan.

C. 1950. The reconstruction of Japan had come a long way in five years. *YouTube screen grab.*

The train inched through cities so dense that homes and shops immediately abutted the rail line. Train passengers could often look down into the homes as they passed. Philip saw countless construction sites packed with laborers intent on displacing the rubble of war. Streets teemed with people on foot, bicycle, or streetcar. He may have noticed that draft horses were not driven, but led by footmen.

In the countryside, farmers and their families toiled in rice paddies, tilling every possible square inch with primitive hand tools and animal-drawn plows. It was not uncommon for a famer to wave at a passing train while pausing to urinate on a railroad siding.

Philip's train crossed from the island of Honshu to Kyushu. This was achieved via the Kanmon Railway tunnel, some two and a quarter miles in length. Almost immediately after the tunnel passage, the train passed through Kokura. About three hours later, Philip's ride would terminate at Sasebo, where he and his fellow 34th Regiment replacements disembarked.

Once on the sprawling base at Camp Mower, each man was given a company assignment. Like all the replacements, Philip relied on a platoon sergeant for a practical orientation to the facilities. Billeting was accomplished in former Japanese military barracks renovated by the U.S. Army Corps of Engineers.

The base was home to a broad cross-section of American boys. Every barracks seemed to have at least one Tennessean or Texan. There were always kids from factory towns in Pennsylvania or Ohio, as well as farm boys from Wisconsin, Missouri or Arkansas. California provided Chicanos from the barrios as well as the sons of Okies transplanted from the dustbowl. Hawaii supplied the Army with more enlistments per capita than any other U.S. state or territory. Prominent among these were Nisei, the first U.S.-born children of Japanese immigrants. Wherever they were from, these were boys mostly of modest means, each of whom in his own way benefitted from the structure provided by Army life.

They would have found it curious that Philip was from Washington, D.C.

*Hey, do you know President Truman?*

Prudently, Philip chose not to reveal the fact that his father was a trade union executive and that his family owned several beach cottages.

<<◇>>

In one way, the timing of Philip's arrival at Camp Mower was serendipitous in that his regiment had just returned from a division-wide field exercise. Philip was spared the chore of roughing it in the elements, but at the same time he lost the opportunity to foster teamwork with his colleagues. But as far as preparing the men for warfare (if only hypothetically), the field exercises were of limited value.

Before Philip's arrival, the Eighth Army was forced by defense budget cuts to curtail advanced weapons training and extended maneuvers. Field exercises increased the risk of damage to equipment, which was almost entirely left over from World War II.

If conducted properly, exercises would coordinate infantry movement with long-range artillery and air-to-ground support. The densely populated Japanese landscape was itself a deterrent to such maneuvering. This was especially true for the 34th Regiment at Sasebo which had no space of its own to conduct any live-fire exercises. The regiment would have to "borrow" space from the neighboring 19th Regiment at Inamura, near Beppu. Costs and logistical complications limited the Eighth Army's ability to conduct training with the scale and frequency it would have preferred. Commanders were hard pressed to ward off the troops' boredom.

The Eighth Army attempted to make up some of the gaps in experiential learning by showing lots of training films. Some films discussed weapons, tactics, equipment operations and field sanitation practices. Others tutored the soldiers about the evils of communism and the role of the U.S. in world affairs.

One film by the Defense Department was entitled *Our Job in Japan*, which portrayed the Japanese in a sympathetic light. Yet other films explained how Americans should conduct themselves when moving about in Japanese society. Films and lectures informed soldiers about the consequences of venereal disease. Chaplains counseled abstinence and chastity. Meanwhile, doctors issued instruction on the proper use of condoms.

The Army went to great lengths to assure the comfort of troops on occupation duty. Dining halls were stocked with ample quantities of American food. The soldiers lacked only fresh dairy products. Otherwise, they enjoyed comfortable barracks, movie theaters, and libraries stocked with books and recent magazines. Daily radio news broadcasts were piped into various common rooms. Red Cross clubs provided opportunities for well-chaperoned leisure.

Philip's weekdays were filled with a combination of field training and close-order drill. Cleaning, kitchen patrol and certain other chores were largely delegated to an abundance of cheap and willing local labor.

Soldiers usually had free time on the weekends, when about a third of the troops in good standing could apply for a weekend pass to venture off base and into surrounding communities. The Americans were eager customers for local hospitality and services, so cultural interaction with the Japanese was an immediate consequence. Soldiers practiced street-level diplomacy by simply handing out chewing gum and candy to Japanese kids. But they also sought and found willing companionship with Japanese girls.

With World War II behind them, and with any new tensions seemingly confined to the U.S.-Soviet frontier in central Europe, the U.S. occupation troops in Japan functioned very much like tourists in this exotic land.

By this time, Philip was accustomed to adapting to new environments. Since the beginning of the previous year, he had bunked in a Canadian boarding school, at a YMCA in Chicago, in the reform school on the heights above Georgetown, in the barracks at Fort Knox, and on a sea-going troop ship. All of these settings placed Philip in a communal or "group home" living space, echoing the institutional setting of the orphanage where he spent his earliest years.

# CHAPTER 15

# Babysan

Considering southern Japan's weather, it was fortuitous that Philip Hughes arrived when he did. May and June followed the cool, foggy winters, but presaged the monsoons of late summer and early fall.

As soon as he checked into the barracks at Camp Mower, Philip was entertained by his bunk mates' boasts about the adventures to be found just off base. In a matter of days, with a coveted weekend pass in hand, he would see Sasebo for himself.

Sasebo in May 1950 was rebuilding quickly. The tallest buildings, never more than three stories, were found on the broadest streets. Buildings on side streets were typically one story and even more densely packed. Visual clutter marred most streets with overhead signs and placards competing to catch the eye of pedestrians. While Japanese merchants welcomed business offered by the Australians who shared in post-war occupation duties, Americans were preferred because they were more numerous and had far more money to spend.

Americans quickly learned the proper salutations that Japanese expected as a courtesy. In Japan, one affixes the suffix "-san" to convey respect when addressing someone by name. When lacking a name, one uses a fictive kinship label as a placeholder. Therefore, appending these together, a gentleman becomes *papasan* and a mature lady is *mamasan*. When addressing a young woman, especially one of potential romantic interest, the always-innovative Americans employed the term *babysan*.

Apart from the streetwalkers (or *panpan* in local pidgin parlance) of Sasebo's red light district, the action was at locally-owned clubs, often lit with neon signage. Visiting soldiers found vast quantities of Kirin beer inside the clubs and young, well-coiffured Japanese women both inside and out. The heady mix of youth, alcohol, and testosterone ensured that an off-duty occupation soldier would find a scuffle just as often as he would connect with a Japanese ingénue. To minimize the unrest in Sasebo, the Army deployed large numbers of military police, joined by the Navy's shore patrol.

Late1940s. Entertainment district, Sasebo, Japan. *U.S. Army.*

Women stimulated the market for hospitality in a variety of ways. *Panpan* – legal in Japan – were numerous and offered a wide range of services, ranging from crude to elegant and discreet. A more innocent vocation simply required well-dressed women to work in bars, where they socialized with American patrons in return for a percentage of drink revenues. Clubs like the Tacharsuka and the Casaba featured jazz combos where female vocalists mimicked popular American tunes, singing verses in Japanese and the refrains in English.

Some Japanese families pooled their resources to establish very small inns, catering primarily to soldiers who ventured off their bases to exercise an overnight pass. The inns were similar in concept to today's bed-and-breakfast establishments, but the Japanese business model often included the traditional amenity of a hot bath – a spa-like experience facilitated by one or more female attendants.

Tens of thousands of women across Japan were involved in one facet or another of the hospitality industry, with the direct knowledge and often the encouragement of their families. Whatever their vocation, many young Japanese women were indispensable to their families' subsistence at a time when the economy offered few other means of income. These services were available to occupation troops at astonishingly low prices. Even a teenage American private had enough disposable income to keep a steady "shack gal," pay a houseboy to shine his boots, and have plenty left over to buy as much beer as he pleased. Aside from cash, he had a ration of cigarettes that could be bartered surreptitiously off base in the black market.

By American standards, Japanese women are tiny, averaging five feet, two inches in height, and are often under 100 pounds. In a word, they are *dainty*. A homesick American boy might have wished for longer legs and fuller bosoms, but a Japanese girl could melt his heart with her egg-shaped face and delicate features set in smooth, clear skin.

The typical young adult Japanese woman could, hypothetically, satisfy her clothing needs in the teen section of a North American department store. Having limited resources, however, she scanned American magazines for cues to hairstyles and clothing. She shared these images with a local dressmaker who then tailored the appropriate garment from bulk fabric within two or three days. A nice Japanese girl in 1950 might venture out in a cardigan and a pleated skirt.

Western footware, however, was not as easy to obtain or duplicate. While a few women managed to find high-heeled shoes, they were more likely – and probably preferred – to wear the *geta*, a traditional sandal that was a sort of combination flip-flop and clog. Instead of stockings, she wore *tabi*, which were like ankle-high socks with reinforced soles and the big toe articulated to accommodate the *geta*.

When dating, the young Japanese woman was quiet, demure, and deferential to her male companion. She was also observant and alert, adeptly reading her companion's facial expressions.

May 1952. Tachikawa, Japan. U.S. enlisted military men fraternizing with Japanese girls. Which fellow is the odd-man out? *National Archives and Records Administration.*

The young adults of post-war Japan came of age at a time of unprecedented social change. A root cause was the American-led reconstruction, which purposely tackled politics, economics, and culture all at once. Western democratic ideals explicitly released Japanese women from the confines of old traditions. Implementation of these ideals was propelled by the screening of imported American movies. Japanese women flocked to theaters to enjoy romance films which so often depicted kissing protagonists – a cinematic experience that had been entirely off limits under the auspices of Japan's erstwhile military culture.

Given unprecedented freedom and responsibility, young women began to imagine new and exciting trajectories for their lives. Fraternization with the American occupation troops further catalyzed Japanese awareness of the possibilities embedded in American technologies and cultural trappings.

A lot can be communicated between young people of the opposite sex, even when lacking a common spoken language. Social connections between occupation soldiers and the young women of Japan were initiated and maintained largely through gestures and facial expressions. Even though they were anxious to connect with American boys, these girls were hardly aggressive. They knew how, with mannered innocence, to subtly invite a boy's advance using no more than a smile or stifled giggle.

Few Japanese girls could speak more than a handful of words in English, and those were often misapplied. A girl might ask, "How long you stay Japan?" What she really meant was "How long *have you been* in Japan?" Having a partial command of each other's language allowed the Americans and the Japanese to fill in the gaps with a sense of humor.

Linguistic barriers probably ensured that Japanese-American unions evolved quickly to a state of intimacy. Made mute by language differences, these couples were forced to communicate by tactile means from the start, encumbered by little if any dialogue.

Her name – Mitsuko? Kyoko? Sachiko? – has long since been forgotten. She was young, certainly, but still perhaps a few years older than Philip. The Second World War left an indelible impact on her family. It might have been the loss of a brother. Her father. Their home. She was scarred by the past, burdened by the present, and unsure of her future. She was like many other young Japanese women who found themselves on the frontline of post-war reconstruction. Both she and Philip were motivated to connect for a mix of reasons. They shared a mutual need… for someone.

It is neither correct nor fair to characterize her as a prostitute. Post-war Japan begat a more complex dynamic. With a mix of emotions, she was resigned to interaction with the Americans. There were probably others before Philip.

In their initial conversation, they were fully tasked with simply learning to pronounce each other's name. Her native phonemic capacity allowed her to say "Phirrip." How well did Philip do with *her* name? During subsequent meetings, they could take in a movie at Camp Mower's theater, or they would hold hands for a stroll through the park where spring blossoms were fully resplendent.

The Japanese loved to take and collect photographs. Philip ensured that he and his girlfriend would exchange pictures. He took her shopping, picking up the tab for goods that she brought home for herself or the rest of her family. As other Japanese women did, she wrapped her purchases in a *furoshiki*, a silk scarf that allowed her to carry a surprising volume of goods by hand.

A monogamous relationship was easier for her to manage, in a purely logistical sense. She assured Philip, in the hybrid linguistics of the occupation era, that he was *onrii*, the equivalent of "only" or the "only one," and thus the exclusive recipient of her affections. She would be reassured if Philip declared that she was *ichiban*, or "number one." Their relationship was a cheerful blend of pragmatism and convenience, yet devoid of guile. She conveyed gratitude with a heartfelt *domo arigato* – thank you very much – but that was not all.

Being Japanese, and therefore informed by Buddhist ideology, her concept of sex was more permissive compared to the morals observed by western culture with its Abrahamic underpinnings. Her society saw sexual pleasure not as a taboo, but rather as a gift to be enjoyed. This allowed Philip, like thousands of other teenaged soldiers in Japan, to completely overhaul his American expectations of courtship. A boy who had yet to even kiss a girl back home often found himself having sex within hours of meeting an accommodating *babysan*.

These encounters were repeated thousands of times during the U.S. occupation of Japan. Philip and his girlfriend would seek space at an inn, where an affable *mamasan* welcomed them. They were required to remove their shoes at the door. Philip didn't have to worry about his shoes being stolen. The Japanese did not care for laced leather footware, and besides, most men would have found his shoes far too big to fit.

Directed to the rear of the inn, Philip and his girlfriend stripped for a traditional Japanese bath. There, she employed a tiny wash basin with soap and a rag for rinsing the two of them before they submerged in a hot tub to soak together. Accustomed to crowded living quarters, she displayed a lack of modesty that Philip must have found astonishing.

Behind a sliding door adjoining the bath area was a small, tidy room that offered privacy. A patchwork of tatami rice mats lined the floor, with an immaculately clean bedroll spread over them. Other furnishings, while perhaps scant, certainly included a charcoal-burning hibachi perched on an insulated mat. Employed as an appliance more than a space heater, it was useful for warming the hands, heating a pot of tea, or for lighting cigarettes. On cooler evenings, occupants of a room would interact by sitting cross-legged immediately around the hibachi.

To stimulate some semblance of conversation, she asked to peruse Philip's wallet. As the other Japanese girls did, she may have blithely noted how much money was present, but she was also genuinely curious about the family photos and cards that he might have carried.

It was in a setting like this that she inevitably surrendered to sex, becoming Philip's teacher even as she was expanding her own vocabulary of intimacy. She obtained edification, yes, and pleasure, but also assured the continuation of Philip's benefaction. He learned to say *domo arigato*.

The relationship continued through May and into June 1950. Having never driven an automobile nor attended even a high school prom, Philip enjoyed the benefits of manhood without its commensurate responsibilities.

He was still only 17 years old.

# CHAPTER 16

# A Brand New War

We are closer to world peace now than at any time in the last three years. *U.S. President Harry S. Truman, June 1949*

W hile still warm, Kyushu weather becomes increasingly wet throughout the spring, as the winds and currents culminate in the monsoons of late summer. Near the end of June, an anomaly of cool, foggy air could prevail for a bit if the conditions were just right. These episodes produced a climate not unlike the one at Monterey, along the central California coast.

On Sunday, June 25, 1950, the rain that fell on Kyushu throughout the day was sufficient to suspend regimental baseball games. By that evening, young American enlisted men were staggering back to Camp Mower from weekend passes. Many sergeants and junior officers – men mostly in their 30s – had dependents with them in base housing; these families were cleaning up after dinner and preparing their kids for bed.

This was when news started to filter in describing an incursion of South Korea by opposing elements from the Soviet-controlled north.

A single, official announcement from the appropriate authority was not forthcoming that night. In Tokyo, General MacArthur's aides refrained from waking him, holding the news until morning. There were confusing snippets on the radio, while rumors were spread by enlisted staff coming off-duty from headquarters. Many young soldiers failed to hear about it that night. Among those who did, only a few even knew where Korea was.

To be fair, border incursions across the 38th parallel that separated the two Koreas were nothing new, and they seemed to end as quickly as they began. It had not yet occurred to anyone at Camp Mower that they could become involved in any way.

In true military fashion, orders began to manifest from the top down in reaction to events in Korea. On June 26th, the United Nations' Security Council issued a resolution that condemned the incursion, calling for a cease fire. Of course, the resolution did nothing to stop the North Koreans, but it did pave the way for the mobilization of U.S. military forces to come to the aid of South Korea. On the 27th, President Harry Truman authorized the use of U.S. military air and sea assets to directly support South Korean (ROK) troops attempting to hold back the North Korean People's Army (NKPA). Still, the North Korean onslaught continued against ineffectual resistance.

When they began their invasion, the NKPA dispatched seven infantry divisions plus an armored brigade, some 135,000 men, across the 38th parallel. They rapidly closed in on Seoul, the capital city of South Korea, a mere 30 miles from the border. Opposing the NKPA were four infantry divisions fielding a total of about 95,000 ROK troops. Not only were the NKPA more numerous, they were equipped with superior weaponry and had many more battle-experienced men among their ranks.

By June 28, Seoul was surrendered to the NKPA. Then by June 30, over 44,000 ROK troops were dead, wounded, or captured. The NKPA continued to move south. All of South Korea was on the verge of capitulation.

Events in Korea presented the United States – and President Truman in particular – a dilemma without precedent. North Korean aggression was an affront to the free world, and by extension, to the newly created United Nations, an organization intended to foster international cooperation before conflict. America's vested interest in the success of the U.N. required mutual cooperation among member nations.

For Truman, the situation provided both political and practical constraints. He could not declare war without an act of Congress. The North Koreans were enabled by the Soviet Union, by now armed with atomic weapons that threatened western Europe. A U.S. declaration of war could hasten another world war.

Truman's advisors quickly devised a measured response – not a war, but a "police action" sanctioned by the U.N., which sought to bring an end to the conflict in Korea. By virtue of their proximity to the Korean peninsula, the U.S. occupation forces in Japan became the vanguard of the U.N. response.

1951. Wake Island. President Harry S. Truman (1884-1972, right), and General Douglas MacArthur (1880-1964) clashed over the jurisdictional domains of their respective positions, but both jointly and ultimately "owned" U.S. strategy for the early conduct of the Korean War. *U.S. Army, Harry S. Truman Library and Museum.*

The order to mobilize an American military commitment to Korea fell to General Douglas MacArthur, commander of U.S. Army Forces in the Far East. Deployment of troops was delegated down a step to General Walton Walker, commander of the U.S. Eighth Army headquartered in Yokohama.

Walker, age 60, was a short, pugnacious, bowling ball of a man from Texas whose army experience dated back to the Veracruz Expedition of 1914. He served as a corps commander in Europe during 1944-45 under George S. Patton. Despite a fondness for alcohol, Walker demanded spit-and-polish decorum of his headquarters staff. Their helmets, jeeps, and weapons were to be kept clean and shined at all times.

Among the assets at Walker's disposal were the four divisions then performing occupation duties in Japan. Walker's approach was cautious yet confident. He initially fulfilled MacArthur's direction by dispatching only the 24th Infantry Division to Korea – and then only in pieces.

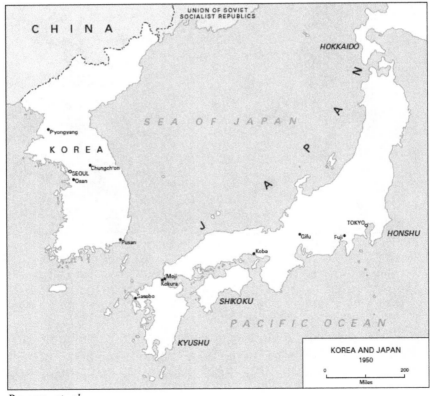

*Bowers, et. al.*

96

Incremental deployment reflected the limitations of Korea's seaports and its few, very rough air fields. The Eighth Army traded a magnitude of men and assets for the speed of their deployment.

A smattering of Eighth Army personnel had some first-hand knowledge of Korea. Such men were concentrated mostly in the 7th Infantry Division, elements of which were tasked with occupation of South Korea from 1945 until they were finally withdrawn back to Japan in late 1949. The country they saw, economically gutted by decades of Japanese occupation, was rife with filth and thievery.

Korea was in many ways worse off than Japan. If an American soldier on duty in Japan during the late 1940s ran afoul of his superiors, he might find himself reassigned to a billet in Korea as a form of punishment. A telling sentiment was once scrawled on the chalkboard of a reception center for troops arriving in Japan in the late 1940s: "Fear only three things: gonorrhea, diarrhea, and Korea."

Yet the American occupation troops during the late 1940s viewed Korea through a flawed perspective. They saw only the consequences of former colonial exploitation, manifested as an imbalanced economy and a crippled civilization. By the end of the 20th century, South Korea would become a stable and even enviable member of the world community. The path to South Korea's transformation began only in the wake of the war that the Americans entered at the end of June 1950.

Major General William F. Dean was seemingly perfect to lead the initial American Army expedition in Korea. After compiling an admirable record as a division commander during World War II, Dean was appointed to the Far East where he played a pivotal role as military governor of South Korea immediately subsequent to Japanese occupation. He had overseen the 24th Division since October 1949.

Tall, lean and athletic, the 50-year-old son of an Illinois dentist eschewed the pomp and circumstance of high rank. Despite having the privilege of using staff cars, Dean was more inclined to walk to his appointments whenever possible. Aides said he was "his own best shoe-shiner."

A preponderance of attributes secured Dean's fate as leader of the first American forces committed to action in Korea: he had combat experience, he was familiar with the country, and his headquarters in Japan were closest to the Korean peninsula. Orders received by Dean's headquarters on July 1 were terse and vague:

> Advance at once upon landing with delaying force in accordance with the situation, to the north by all possible means, contact the enemy now advancing south from Seoul towards Suwon and delay his advance.

Dean had virtually no intelligence at his disposal. What were the size and organization of the enemy forces? How were they armed? Were Russian troops comingled with the NKPA? Delay them for how long… and then what? But of what concern was this to the top military brass? After all, this was the *United States Army*, an organization that emerged victorious from World War II. What challenge could the little North Korean army possibly pose?

The crisis in Korea began to impact Camp Mower. An immediate priority for the U.S. military was to evacuate American and allied non-combatants from Korea. Because Camp Mower was close to the port of Sasebo, which in turn was the facility closest to Korea, the troops of the 34th Regiment were ordered on June 29 to clear out their barracks to accommodate the anticipated arrival of displaced diplomats, missionaries, and the like. Once removed from the barracks, the troops began to set up tents for themselves on the parade grounds, but this arrangement lasted for all of one day. All passes were canceled. The bars in Sasebo fell silent.

Proximity to Korea did not constitute readiness on the part of the 24th Infantry Division as a whole. As of the previous May

30, the division's combat effectiveness rating was only 65 percent – the lowest of all four divisions in Japan. Few troops with World War II combat experience remained in the ranks. Defense budget cuts assured that infantry regiments were reduced to two-thirds strength, while armor complements were similarly redacted. Accordingly, the Eighth Army transferred over 3,700 men from neighboring divisions, swelling the ranks of the 24th to 16,000.

The 24th Division's three understrength regiments were scattered across southern Japan as a result of space limitations. The 19th Infantry Regiment was at Beppu, the 21st at Kumamoto, and Philip Hughes's 34th was in Sasebo. Many of the Division's supporting engineering, quartermaster, and ordinance units were inconveniently located to the north on Japan's main island of Honshu. Mobilizing these assets as a full division would be difficult.

Finding troops was an exercise in compromise and expedience. Through the summer of 1950, Eighth Army personnel staff in Japan performed "Operation Flushout," combing through personnel rosters for cooks, drivers, mechanics, military police, and others. With the stroke of a pen, they would be converted into infantrymen and shipped off to Korea. Military police escorted inmates from the stockade, removing their handcuffs only as regiments took custody of these men and restored them to duty. Some of the personnel clerks would find their own names added to the roster.

As a fully mechanized organization, the division employed some 4,773 vehicles, including jeeps, trucks and trailers of various capacities. The men required food, fuel, clothing, tool kits, radios, medical supplies, binoculars, flashlights, tents, and lumber with related construction supplies. Spools of rope, chains, barbed wire, and communication lines were pulled from storage. Facilities for cooking, bathing, laundry and clerical functions were modularly configured for easy on- and off-loading from truck cargo beds. Finally, there were weapons, including grenades, pistols, rifles, bazookas, mortars and machine guns, artillery cannon, and ammunition for each of these.

The good news for the 24th Division was that a lot of equipment was at its disposal. The bad news was that most of these items, including the food, dated back to 1945. Huge stockpiles of materials – both new and battle-worn – had been amassed on Okinawa, Guam, and other critical supply points in the South Pacific in anticipation of the invasion of Japan that never transpired. During the years leading up to 1950, the Eighth Army rummaged through these depots, retrieving material for rehabilitation, storage, and eventual use in Japan. This meant, for example, that some men first sent to Korea were issued rifles that were still encased in greasy cosmoline while others received dirty and broken weapons retrieved from the battlefields of the last war. Rehabilitated vehicles ran rough and were prone to breakdown, taxing the patience of mechanics. All of these items, regardless of their wear or neglect, had to be shuttled to the port of Sasebo for embarkation to Korea.

1951. Sasebo, Japan. This is the U.S. Army pier from which the 34th Infantry Regiment departed Japan on board the *Takasago Maru*, enroute to Korea on July 2, 1950. *Photo by Maj. C.B. White, U.S. Army, via Doug Price collection.*

Japanese locals turned out on the first two days of July 1950 to cheer the impromptu parade of trucks that hauled troops and equipment from their bases to the docks at Sasebo. Some of the Americans pondered this: were the Japanese grateful for protection from communist aggression, or were they happy to see the occupiers leave?

100

Few if any men could contact girlfriends to say good-bye. Poor weather only added to the troops' gloom.

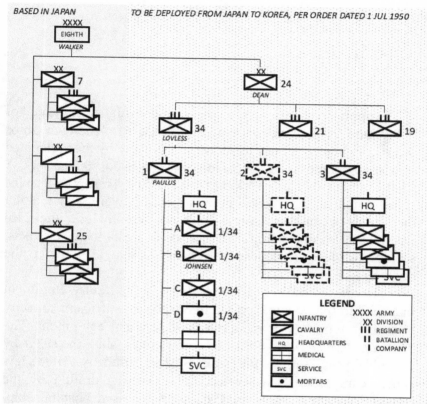

This figure shows the table of organization for the U.S. Eighth Army, and in particular, its components that provided the initial American military commitment to the Korean War in 1950. Budget cutbacks at the time forced the elimination of corps level (XXX) command structures. Similarly, units depicted with dotted lines are those reduced to "on-paper only" status. Private Philip Thomas Hughes deployed as a "light weapons infantry man." At this time, he was a member of B Company, first battalion of the 34th Infantry Regiment, 24th Infantry Division of the U.S. Eighth Army. See Technical Note 1, "Explanation of U.S. Army Unit Organization and Leadership Ranks." Also, see Technical Note 2, "Documentation of Philip Thomas Hughes's Military Service."

# CHAPTER 17

# Pusan

Shipping capacity was scarce in southern Japan at the end of June 1950. The once vast armada of American ships constructed for use in World War II were by then relegated to storage or "mothball" fleets in various U.S. coastal harbors. A small number of hard-working Military Sea Transport Service ships remained in service, but most of these were busy making their trans-oceanic crossings. With no time to lose, the 24th Division's transportation staff worked their local contacts, seeking to lease Japanese merchant vessels to transfer the division to Korea.

The transportation officer for the 34th Infantry Regiment managed to find a ship, berthed in Sasebo, of sufficient capacity to carry a regiment of men and their personal equipment. The *Takasago Maru* was built as a passenger ship in 1937 by Mitsubishi Nagasaki for the Osaka Soshen Company. After a few short years of civilian service, the liner was drafted by the Imperial Japanese Navy in 1941 to serve as a hospital ship. Accordingly, it was painted white with large, red crosses, one on each side of her hull and on both sides of her two smoke stacks. These non-combatant markings, plus a measure of luck, ensured that the *Takasago Maru* was one of the very few Japanese merchant ships to survive World War II. The ship completed a series of post-war cruises to the Philippines, Indochina, and other ports across the far east to bring Japanese troops back home. Reverted to civilian control and by 1950 moored at a warehouse pier, the ship and her domestic crew saw sporadic use. They welcomed a charter from the 34th Regiment.

Before departing Camp Mower by truck for the port of Sasebo, the men of the 34th Regiment were issued rifles, side arms, and ammunition. Now outfitted for field operations, each man wore combat fatigues consisting of herringbone twill dungarees, an equally bulky field jacket, a helmet, double-buckle boots, and an array of belted carrying pouches. In addition, the soldiers each shouldered a duffle bag for clothing, bed rolls, and personal effects. The 34th Regiment's vehicles – up to a hundred cargo trucks and almost as many jeeps and trailers – were being shipped separately, and would arrive the next day.

Late 1945. Manila Harbor. Five years later, on July 2, 1950, troops of the U.S. Army's 34th Infantry Regiment embarked for Pusan, Korea aboard the *Takasago Maru*, a vessel previously employed as a hospital ship by the Imperial Japanese Navy during World War II. *Travelserver.net.*

They queued their way up the *Takasago Maru*'s single, narrow stair during the pre-dawn hours of Sunday, July 2, continuing into the dim confines of the ship. The ship's floors retained marble tiles dating back to its days as a true passenger liner. The cabins, however, had been stripped bare of contents.

Many men opted to perch themselves topside on the wooden deck. Comfort eluded them, but the men made do for the anticipated 15-hour passage.

By 7:00 a.m., the ship weighed anchor. Its steam boilers revved up as the crew retrieved the mooring lines from their bollards. The 34th Regiment's headquarters morning report recorded the ship's cast-off time as 7:15 a.m. A half hour later, the *Takasago Maru* cleared the harbor. Wind whistled through its rigging as the ship gained speed and left Japan in its wake.

The ship's path to the Korean coast bent around the island of Tsushima. Few of the Americans were aware of it, but the bottom of the straits through which they passed were littered with no less than 21 of Tsar Nicholas II's ships, sunk in 1905 as the result of a disastrous encounter with the Japanese Navy during the Russo-Japanese War. The young Americans on the *Takasago Maru* were preoccupied by what awaited them in the very near future.

The men could smell Korea before they even saw it. Prevailing winds from the peninsula carried the stench of human waste – the traditional farmers' fertilizer of choice.

It was almost 9:00 p.m. as the *Takasago Maru* approached the harbor at Pusan. The first view of Korea for the men on deck was the jagged ridgeline of the Taebaek Mountains, backlit by the setting sun. These mountains dropped quickly to the narrow coastal plain. Lights from the port city of Pusan sparkled above the waterline.

Pusan's harbor infrastructure could accommodate up to 24 ocean-going vessels at once. No other South Korean port boasted nearly as much capacity. Pusan also offered the best infrastructure for transferring bulk cargo from ship to rail. Accordingly, Pusan was crucial for importing the assets needed for South Korea's defense.

On the bridge of the *Takasago Maru*, the ship's pilot aligned the bow with a red marker some 35 yards inland from the dock. The ship scraped a series of pilings along the pier and ground to a halt. An American harbormaster drove onto the dock in an orange jeep; he would orient the ship's crew for subsequent unloading of passengers.

August 6, 1950. Pusan, Korea. Troops of the U.S. 23rd Infantry Regiment have just arrived from Bremerton, Washington. They await complete off-loading of their cargo ship before proceeding inland. Note the cramped dock space. *U.S. Army.*

This pier was not configured for disembarkation via descending walkway. Instead, the troops would exit from a row of water-tight cargo hatches just above the waterline. These hatches – each 12-feet square in dimension – were secured to the interior of the hull by a number of latches, or "dogs." A crewman came through with a sledgehammer, deftly whacking each dog 90 degrees to loosen it. With the hatches removed, the view revealed a series of piles set in the water along the length of the pier in rows that mimicked steps. Upon exiting the ship, the men used these piles to step up to the pier.

By 11:30 p.m., the men began a six-mile march to Camp Hialeah, a former horse racing track that the Japanese had repurposed into an army base many years before. The men pitched their tents for the night there. Their sleep was challenged by the tinkling sound of old tin cans strung on a wire around the camp perimeter – a crude but effective early-warning system devised some years ago by Americans from the 7th Division to ward off thieves. In the aftermath of the occupation, no one had bothered to dismantle it.

The next day was Monday, July 3. The men of the 34th spent the morning organizing equipment. Many soldiers had overburdened themselves with personal effects; the excess was directed into storage. Even when pared down to combat necessities, each infantryman carried 60 to 80 pounds of equipment, mostly on his back. Meanwhile, the regiment's vehicles arrived in Pusan. Transportation officers sought the means to get everyone to the front. Railroads were the most practical option.

Late on Tuesday afternoon, the infantrymen exited Camp Hialeah on foot, heading for the train depot located a couple miles to the west. This march provided the men with their first good look at Pusan. The air was at times thick with the smoke from cooking fires, stoked in the many lots occupied by a growing number of refugees displaced from the north by the encroaching communist invasion.

Pedestrians and bicycles teemed through Pusan's streets. The few automobiles were old and wobbly. If any of the American troops were from Atlanta, they would have been surprised to recognize Georgia Power trolley cars from their home town – recently bequeathed as economic recovery gifts to Korea – lumbering along the street rails of Pusan.

As in every Korean city, the infrastructure of Pusan was built by the Japanese for the convenience of Japan. Services of direct benefit to the Koreans were scarce. This was most evident in the lack of sanitary sewer capacity. As he marched through the city, Philip was struck not so much by the number of children, but by their capacity to play with little or no resources. These children had streets for their playground and gutters for their toilet.

At the end of their marching tour, the regiment arrived at the Pusan train station. There they found five trains with Korean crews at their disposal. These featured a mix of coaches and flatcars for carrying vehicles. Curiously, amidst all the commotion, the Americans encountered a number of Korean boys on the train platforms with their shoe shine kits, awaiting patrons. Many of them paired their service, one boy per shoe.

Ships from Japan disgorged more men and supplies throughout the day. The Eighth Army sought to fill the 34th Regiment's understrength ranks by transferring in certain numbers of troops from the units remaining in Japan. Thanks to Army culture, this was an opportunity for the other units to rid themselves of the slackers and malcontents from their ranks.

Once in Pusan, these replacements caught up with the 34th at the train station. Their numbers included at least nine privates and two sergeants. They brought rumors to spread; to thwart this, the officers attempted to brief the men with what little official information they had. Some of the officers assured that they were embarking on a "police action." No one was quite sure what that meant.

At General Dean's direction, organizational changes continued even as the men milled about the railyard waiting to board northbound trains. Dean anticipated a shuffling of his field-grade officers, knowing that some incumbents would need to be replaced by officers with proven combat experience.

The shake-up of leaders impacted Philip's chain of command. For now, the commander of the 34th Regiment was Colonel Jay B. Lovless, a 49-year-old logistician who had held this position only for a couple of months. One of his subordinates, Lieutenant Colonel Lawrence Paulus, was relieved of his command of the 34th's first battalion. His replacement was an officer that Lovless had never met before. Thirty-one-year old Lieutenant Colonel Harold "Red" Ayres was a Louisianan decorated for his service in Italy during World War II.

Among the rifle companies within first battalion was Philip Hughes's Baker Company, led by 1st Lieutenant Raymond Johnsen of Chicago. All of five feet, five inches tall, he was also a decorated veteran of World War II, having won a Silver Star in 1943 for "conspicuous gallantry and intrepidity" during combat action in the South Pacific.

The troops began boarding the trains around 9:00 p.m. For Philip Hughes, the impending trip would vaguely resemble his runaway excursion to Chicago just one year earlier. He was departing a coastal city by rail, headed generally northwest on a double-tracked right-of-way through a series of rocky hills and tunnels. Rather than the Alleghenies, his train would climb through the Taebaek mountains. In place of Harper's Ferry, Cumberland, and Pittsburgh, he would encounter Taegu, Taejon, and P'yongt'aek. Also, the Korean coach offered wooden bench seating, a far cry from the reclining, upholstered seats on the B&O's air-conditioned Columbian. Here, the soldiers had no choice but to open the coach windows to get some relief from the lingering heat and the stench of their own sweat. When encountering tunnels, smoke and cinders from the locomotives wafted into the coaches' open windows.

The railroad was less than a century old, but it followed the same route to Korea's interior that had been used by invading forces all through history.

While passing through Taejon, some 165 miles from Pusan, the Americans saw a lot of ROK troops milling about, apparently disorganized and lacking equipment.

Philip's train continued northward.

<<◇>>

Preceding the 34th Regiment's arrival in Korea was an advance force prescribed by Eighth Army leadership. "Task Force Smith" was so named for its commander, 34-year-old Lieutenant Colonel Charles "Brad" Smith, a West Pointer and a veteran of World War II's Pacific theater. Smith's foray into Korea employed a reinforced company of about 540 men detailed from the 21st Infantry Regiment with a partial complement of artillery.

The composition of this force reflected the need to move quickly – by air – which in turn was restricted by Korea's rough airfields, which quickly deteriorated under the weight of heavily-loaded aircraft. For practical purposes, then, Task Force Smith was lightly equipped. Over half the troops were under the age of 20 – soldiers, yes, but generally undertrained and unprepared.

As long as their opponents lacked superior troop numbers and armament, Task Force Smith was expected to provide an effective roadblock to the North Korean incursion. A formation under an American flag would, in MacArthur's words, pose "an arrogant display of strength" from which North Korean troops would supposedly recoil in fear. MacArthur's tacit hope was that the enemy would perceive the few Americans initially deployed in Korea as the vanguard of the vast military juggernaut that had won World War II.

The North Koreans were neither fooled nor intimidated by the meager force of Americans they encountered.

Having already taken Seoul, the capital of South Korea, the North Korean People's Army advanced southward toward Osan on July 5. Just north of there, Task Force Smith, the front line of American resistance, was dug-in on a couple of rain-soaked hilltops. Almost 5,000 NKPA troops advanced on this position behind a spearhead of over 30 top-notch Russian-built T-34 tanks. The few American weapons that could effectively stop tanks were quickly neutralized. The experienced and battle hardened NKPA forces poured around and through the Americans, killing some, capturing others, and causing a panicked rout of the remainder. The dazed survivors fled south, leaving behind equipment and wounded men that they could not carry.

Some 40 percent of the task force was lost – either killed, captured, or wounded. In return for their efforts, Task Force Smith delayed the NKPA advance for approximately seven hours. Their roadblock gave the 34th Regiment time to set up its line of defense to the south at P'yongt'aek.

June 29, 1950. Seoul, South Korea. Russian-built T-34 tank of the North Korean People's Army. Americans fighting during the first weeks of the Korean War found T-34s to be rugged, fast, heavily armored, and virtually unstoppable. *http://ysfine.com/kowar/tanks.html*

This first engagement was the model for the U.S. Army's strategy in Korea throughout the summer of 1950. The burden of checking the NKPA's advance fell almost strictly to ground forces. The best these units could do was to delay the enemy's advance. Their orders were to hold until threatened by envelopment, then withdraw and regroup to form another line of resistance. This approach would implicitly trade land – and lives – for the time the Eighth Army needed to ship more men and armaments from Japan into the port at Pusan.

# CHAPTER 18

# P'yongt'aek

General Dean's mission to halt the advancing North Korean People's Army would be helped or hindered by the features of the Korean landscape. A topography map revealed what Dean needed: a bottleneck that limited the enemy's ability to maneuver astride his main avenue of advance.

Such a place was in the vicinity of P'yongt'aek, a fishing port south of Osan. To the west was a tidal marsh that quickly yielded to the Yellow Sea; ten miles to the east were the Charyeong mountains of central Korea. Given the rout of Task Force Smith on July 5, the axis above P'yongt'aek became the main line of U.S. Army resistance to the NKPA.

The 34th Infantry Regiment, numbering just under 2,000 men, would be responsible for this ten-mile front, deployed in two battalions – those being the *first* and the *third*, as the *second* existed only on paper. Their numbers were too small to fortify a continuous line of defense.

Dean therefore deployed one battalion each to cover the two roadways leading south toward the interior. Below these two points, the landscape opened up from west to east. Holding the line at P'yongt'aek was critical to containing the enemy with the limited resources available to the 34th Regiment.

On the night of July 4-5, while Task Force Smith was digging in some 15 miles to the north, the 34th Regiment pulled into the P'yongt'aek rail yard, which was still smoldering from mistaken bombardment a few days earlier by a flight of fighter-bombers from the Royal Australian Air Force's 77 Squadron. Amidst the smoking wreckage were some demolished ammunition trucks and dead bodies to which no one had the time or resources to attend.

The service company immediately unloaded the regiment's vehicles. The regiment's transfer from rail to road was impeded by a large number of Korean civilians encamped in and about the train station. These were refugees from points north seeking to escape communist control. Because the military had commandeered almost all rail capacity, these people would continue southward on foot the next morning, clogging the same roads needed by the Army. Some of the Americans noted the many male refugees of fighting age. Why weren't these men in the South Korean army?

July 1950. Civilian refugees flee the war zone. Refugees clogged the roads throughout South Korea in 1950-51, often with clandestine enemy infiltrators among them. The man in the front bears the ingenious A-frame, allowing him to carry enormous loads on his back. *U.S. Army, Harry S. Truman Library and Museum.*

The Americans piled into trucks that took them farther north on a rough and rain-slicked road, constructed on levees that traversed rice paddies. It was not at all encouraging to pass a number of trucks overturned in the reddish-brown muck below.

The first battalion deployed about two and a half miles north of P'yongt'aek, where one road cut across rice paddies that separated two hills. The men spent the day on July 5 digging into their assigned positions.

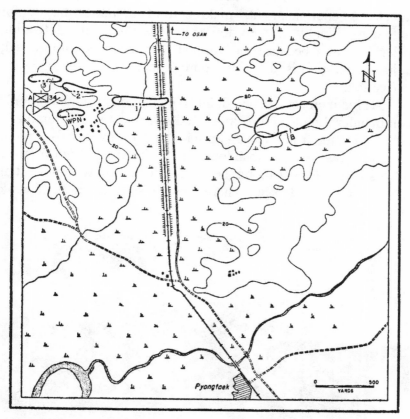

Initial deployment of first battalion, 34th Infantry Regiment in Korea, July 5, 1950. Note the location of B (Baker) Company, to the right (east) of the road and rail corridor. *Center of Military History, United States Army.*

The western side of the road was Able Company's responsibility. Baker Company dug in on high ground over a half mile to the east. Charlie Company remained in reserve to the rear, in P'yongt'aek. Meanwhile, the third battalion deployed ten miles to the east, which is where the other north-south road ran through the town of Ansong.

High ground is always the preferred posture for the defense of a military position. For one, the defender enjoys an enhanced view of the surrounding terrain. Also, an upward slope slows the attacker's encroachment, making him a better target for defenders. Finally, a steep down-slope facilitates the defending rifleman's aim because the vertical dimension is compressed; adjustments to his aim are more concerned with sideways correction.

As his men established defensive positions, first battalion's commander, Lieutenant Colonel Red Ayres, set up his command post behind the front line in a farm house. This modest four-room structure was recently abandoned by its family, but not by their domestic livestock. Among these were ducks that waddled out of the mud and into the hut where Ayres's staff set up their work space.

1951. South Korea. No place like home. Those humble, hand-made peasant dwellings that were not destroyed by the war were often commandeered as needed for shelter by combatants on both sides. *www.koreanwar-educator.org.*

Platoon leaders scanned the landscape for crags, rises, and other features that provided natural concealment; troops were dispersed accordingly. To prepare the ground for defense, the soldiers created barricades from logs, rocks, and the like. When such materials were lacking, they would have to dig foxholes instead.

The rain intensified as evening approached. Some of the men donned their standard-issue rain ponchos. They found how difficult it is for a man to sling a shovel around while cloaked in a knee-length tarpaulin. Once at rest, the soldier could pull the poncho's neckline up over his chin to foil the wetness. It was only a matter of time, however, before the rain invaded a seam in the poncho's rubberized fabric. The wearer was inevitably forced to endure a rivulet of cold water running down his back. The foxholes began to fill with rain water.

Sergeants wandered about the men, checking on weapon readiness and offering words of encouragement. Each man had just under 100 rounds of ammunition. There were no grenades.

At this point, there wasn't much to do but watch refugees streaming southward on the road below them. With rare exception, Korean civilians were draped in white robes with baggy white trousers. This sartorial standard was derived from Korea's monarchical traditions. In ancient times, white clothing was worn to indicate mourning over the death of kings. Each royal passing required a mourning period of 30 years. Given the short life spans of Korean royalty, the populace found itself perpetually dressed in white, a custom that lingered into the 20th century.

At about 2:00 or 3:00 the next morning, the men who were not on watch were awakened by a loud explosion. This was the handiwork of combat engineers, who blew up a bridge located 600 yards north of the first battalion's position.

Dawn arrived with a cold, clammy fog. The men sought breakfast, tearing open C-ration boxes that were date-stamped "1945." By 6:00 a.m., motor rumblings were audible to the north.

Through binoculars, the Americans could see activity just beyond the blown bridge. At first, there was some confusion. By now, commanders throughout the 34th Regiment were vaguely informed of the demise of Task Force Smith. They knew that the 34th was not equipped to stop the NKPA, especially its tanks. Columns of troops became evident through the mist. Was it the remnants of Task Force Smith? Then, the unmistakable outline of tanks appeared. Task Force Smith had no tanks. The identity of the approaching force was now definitive.

The Americans fired first in an exchange that quickly escalated to include machine guns, rifles, and mortars. The NKPA tanks could not yet circumvent the blown bridge, but they could fire on the American positions. Their foot soldiers forded the creek and continued to close in, firing at the Americans with rifles held at the hip.

The first battalion's combat initiation had begun. A crescendo of shouts and weapons discharge rose at once. The smoke and sulfurous aroma of gunpowder mixed with the morning fog. The enemy's bullets zipped and cracked through the air with increasing frequency.

For young, uninitiated American soldiers, the atmosphere was at the very least disconcerting, especially for those who had not fired a weapon since basic training. Many of the boys had forgotten how to correctly assemble and operate their weapons. And only now did some unlucky soldiers discover that their World War II surplus rifles were defective. When attempting to load ammunition clips into their M1s, some soldiers had their thumbs smashed by the rifle's powerful spring-loaded bolt.

In the confusion of a firefight, an untested soldier wrestling with an unfamiliar weapon could easily lose awareness of the field of battle around him. Men stirred within the defensive perimeter. Runners sought to retrieve more ammunition from crates just behind the line. Men shifted from one fighting position to another at the command of sergeants, allowing them to concentrate firepower on encroaching threats. Medics crisscrossed the position responding to the cries of wounded men. Communication was necessarily vociferous as men barked back and forth through the din of weapons fire. *Was the sergeant yelling at me, or someone else?* Confusion compromised the integrity of the defensive force, providing commensurate advantage to the attackers.

On the west side of the road, particularly in the rice paddies, the NKPA were on top of Able Company's perimeter before the defenders knew it. Lieutenant Colonel Ayres could see from his vantage point that the enemy threatened to outflank and overrun his battalion. At around 6:30 a.m. he radioed orders to Able and Baker Companies to initiate a combat withdrawal. This called for movement of one platoon at a time to a pre-determined rallying point while the rest sustained fire against the attacking foe. The challenge was to distribute the order to all squads dispersed along the defensive perimeter.

Such a maneuver had not been thoroughly practiced when the troops were back in Japan. Not everyone was aware of the order. Only then did some of Americans suddenly notice that the figures scurrying around them were uniformed not in olive drab, but rather a mustard-brown color. By then, it was too late to withdraw.

With the NKPA's imminent encroachment, panic gripped some of the defenders. Many of those among the withdrawing ranks failed to stop and return fire to cover the next rank. The NKPA encountered kids in their foxholes paralyzed by fear and disbelief at what was happening. Some of these boys were disarmed and taken prisoner; others were killed outright.

On the hill over on the eastern flank, the men of Baker Company were generally better prepared and able to return fire. Their withdrawal was more effective as they came off their hill almost intact and maintained unit integrity as they moved south to regroup at P'yongt'aek.

In contrast, Able Company momentarily disintegrated as it abandoned its dead and wounded along with much of their equipment at the defensive position. Many survivors discarded personal equipment during the southerly retreat. The path of retreat took many men through rice paddies. Either by choice or consequence, some men surrendered their boots to the muck. Officers were appalled to see gaggles of barefoot men bereft of helmets, rifles, and ammunition. It was noon before the first battalion was clear of enemy fire. About one fourth of their number, mostly from Able Company, were killed, missing, or captured.

Baker Company was better off, but not unscathed. Four of its members were not accounted for at the end of the day. Private Ed "Buster" Morrison, a 19-year-old from Ashland, Wisconsin, was killed at his fighting position. Senior among the rest was Sergeant First Class Al Vercolen, age 29, a war veteran from Rochester, New York. In all likelihood, Vercolen and his squad were positioned on Baker Company's forward edge or its eastern flank, farthest from the road. The turmoil and confusion of battle prevented them from receiving (or obeying) the order to pull back. There may have been others in the squad who withdrew before the NKPA cut off their line of retreat.

Remaining with Vercolen were Walter David McNary, an 18-year-old from East Detroit, and 17-year-old Jackie Lee Murdock from Crawfordsville, Indiana. These three were all added to the 34th Regiment's roster just a couple days before, on July 4 at the Pusan train station.

Their unfamiliarity with the command structure and communication style within Baker Company certainly detracted from their effectiveness on the battlefield. Surrounded and outgunned, they opted to surrender. They were corralled with prisoners from Able Company, among the first of over 7,100 Americans who would be taken captive in Korea. The North Koreans did not anticipate taking prisoners, especially Americans, and had no provisions for their care. Captives were herded northward on foot over many weeks into North Korea. Those who survived the brutal trek would be confined for the next three years.

Not one of the Baker Company men captured at P'yongt'aek survived to reach a prison camp, nor were their remains ever recovered.

# CHAPTER 19

# What Have I Gotten Myself Into?

P hilip Hughes, like any other American soldier rushed to Korea in July of 1950, was given only the most cursory explanation of the conflict to which he was committed. Even worse, his leaders provided no warning of the tactics and temperament of the opposing combatants. All they knew was that the nation of South Korea had been invaded, and that American forces were being sent to the rescue.

The origins of the Korean War were sown long before 1950. A country relatively isolated by the sea, Korea's only significant land border is with China. Although China is larger and more populous, it influenced rather than exploited Korea, which has sustained a distinct ethnicity, language, and culture.

Prior to the 20th century, Korean civilization was shaped by a filial aristocracy empowered by land ownership. That dominant class discouraged mercantilism, thus denying most Koreans one of the few practical means for amassing wealth and independence. Accordingly, the vast majority of Koreans subsisted as peasants beholden to a few privileged gentry. This feudalist paradigm left the Korean population ill-prepared at the start of the 20th century to develop the economic infrastructure and technologies needed to keep pace with its aggressive neighbors.

China's position as Korea's dominant neighbor was unchallenged until the 1890s, when Japan and Russia each deployed the sea power needed to assert their imperial aspirations. Korea then became a geographic fulcrum as the three great powers of the Far East sought a regional buffer among each other.

Through the exercise of military might, Japan by 1905 became the hegemonic power of the Far East at the expense of China and Russia. Japan's ascendency was not lost on American leaders who had coincident aspirations in the western Pacific, focused primarily on the Philippine Islands, which the U.S. absorbed as a result of the Spanish-American War.

President Theodore Roosevelt facilitated negotiations leading to the Treaty of Portsmouth, which in 1905 brought the Russo-Japanese war to a close. In the process, Roosevelt bartered an agreement with Japanese Prime Minister Taro Katsura: the U.S. recognized Japan's control over Korea in exchange for Japan's promise to stay away from the Philippines. This arrangement effectively paved the way for a series of Japanese conquests, including Korea, which became a Japanese protectorate in 1905 and then its colony in 1910.

Japan's aspirations were inspired by its want of raw materials combined with its overtly militarist political culture. Through colonial domination, the Japanese sought to extract both human and natural resources from Korea. The only hurdle to these ambitions was the Korean population: the Japanese would displace these people, co-opt their labor, or simply kill them.

Japanese control impacted early 20th century Korea in dramatically different ways. Some Koreans chose the path of armed resistance, while others opted to improve their fortunes through cooperation with Japanese authorities. The Koreans who chose to collaborate with the Japanese did so to varying degrees. Collaboration ranged from the benign – participating in the day-to-day tasks of colonial administration – to the insidious, evidenced by Koreans who functioned as secret police to reveal and destroy thousands of potential dissidents, usually with their families for good measure.

But unlike their peasant counterparts, collaborative Koreans were often individuals who had (or could develop) skills to assist the Japanese as technicians or low-level bureaucrats. For many Koreans, collaboration provided unprecedented access to education and employment, albeit for Japan's ultimate benefit.

The dichotomy of collaboration versus resistance was entrenched by Japan's ongoing regional conquests. The years 1931-32 were pivotal: Japan invaded and annexed Manchukuo (Manchuria), the vast Chinese territory just opposite Korea's northwestern border. Peasants from Korea and China became united in resistance by leaders that espoused communist ideology. Under communism, the resistance movement achieved organizational discipline with a ruthlessness that rivaled that of the Japanese.

In turn, the Japanese escalated their tactics of repression through the 1930s until their final capitulation in 1945. These years honed a generation of Korean peasant warriors for whom lethal force and the expendability of human life were not only routinely accepted, but expected.

The stage for Korea's post-World War II fortunes was irrevocably altered by the Soviet Union's entry into the far-east Asian theater of war. With the cessation of hostilities in Europe in May 1945, Stalin turned his focus to Japan, hoping to renew Russian territorial ambitions dating back to the turn of the century. At the same time, U.S. military planners contemplated invasion of the Japanese home islands as the key to a decisive victory in the Pacific.

American leaders certainly had misgivings about Stalin's goals, but weariness begotten by four years of war led them to acquiesce to Russia's entry, ostensibly to reduce America's combat burden. The anticipated invasion of Japan was rendered moot by Japan's unconditional surrender after U.S. atomic bombs obliterated Hiroshima and Nagasaki.

Allied victory over Japan at the end of World War II presented the challenge of disarming the Japanese military and restoring self-determination to occupied territories like Korea. Anticipating post-war international cooperation and expedience, U.S. leaders proposed a formula for the demilitarization of Japanese-occupied Korea that the Soviet Union readily accepted. Specifically, Korea was arbitrarily divided by the global circle of latitude denoted by the 38th parallel; demilitarization north of the parallel would accrue to the Russians, while territory south of that line would be handled by the Americans.

As Cold War animosities beset U.S.-Soviet relations, Korea became effectively separated into two distinct societies: one defined by its resistance to Japanese domination and the other by its acquiescence. The years 1945-50 saw demographic upheaval in Korea as adherents to the resistance legacy coalesced primarily in the north, while the former collaborationists made their home in the south. Thanks to their stark philosophical differences, these two Korean societies developed deep, mutual animosities and distrust as each side longed to reunite Korea according to its own ideology. Governments on both sides of the border readily used armed force to suppress real or perceived threats of dissonance.

U.S.-Soviet cooperation waned during the late 1940s, as did American access to Korea north of the 38th parallel. Accordingly, America advanced post-war political and economic restitution in Korea by engaging the southerners exclusively. If many South Koreans had resumes tainted by collaboration with the Japanese, it meant little to the Americans in light of emerging Cold War concerns.

Developed under Communist Chinese tutelage, the North Korean People's Army of 1950 drew its leadership, battlefield tactics, and *esprit de corps* from its years of anti-Japanese resistance. Even before the end of World War II, the same communist alliance bore arms against the U.S.-backed Nationalist Chinese forces on mainland China. About one third of the North Korean troops committed to war in June 1950 were combat veterans of the Chinese Civil War of the late 1940s.

Tensions between North and South Korea intensified through 1949 in the form of border clashes and incursions. In effect, the NKPA's invasion of South Korea on June 25, 1950 was an escalation of a Korean civil war that had already begun. The invading NKPA force was well-prepared with weaponry, much of it new, supplied by their Soviet and Chinese mentors. In addition, these troops were deployed with both military and political officers – the latter to indoctrinate and inspire rank-and-file soldiers. NKPA troops were imbued with a sense of purpose that drew on their heritage of resistance and a reliance on lethal force devoid of clemency or mercy.

June 1950. Seoul, South Korea. North Korean People's Army (NKPA) troops on the move. They were physically fit, well trained, experienced, and very resourceful. *http://thekoreanwarof1950-53.weebly.com/the-invasion.html.*

Philip Hughes and the other Americans rushed to Korea in 1950 encountered a tidal wave of refugees that clogged road and rail networks. For the most part, they fled the consequences of regime change. The opposing forces in Korea's civil war shared a common legacy of merciless authoritarianism under decades of Japanese domination. Any change in local authority during Korea's civil war precipitated mortal danger. History taught Koreans not to expect engagement and compromise from their new leaders, but ruthless force in the quelling dissidents, either real or perceived.

The Japanese experience demonstrated how fear and intimidation begat compliance. Communism was even more fearsome, pitting neighbor against neighbor to purge entire families if one individual was even suspected of harboring "anti-revolutionary" sentiments. These dynamics caused thousands of ordinary citizens to abandon their homes before the NKPA's advance. Refugees of all ages, burdened with whatever possessions they could carry, flooded the meager Korean road network, trudging southward toward a place – any place – that was hopefully beyond the communists' reach.

<<<>>>

In Korea, for the first time in history, the American military waged war in a come-as-you-are fashion. There were no months dedicated to the build-up of troop strength and the production of weapons and materiel prior to some monumental and decisive invasion. The 24th Infantry Division deployed units to Korea that were cobbled together, drawing manpower at the last minute from disparate sources. To equip them, quartermasters in Japan drew down stockpiles of surplus assets from World War II. These tools were placed in the hands of soldiers who had little training or motivation to conduct a war.

Meanwhile, back in the United States, the populace never assumed a wartime footing with its dreaded rationing of commodities and diversion of strategic resources. The war in Korea affected policy makers, certain manufacturers, and journalists. A direct impact befell the reservists – mostly World War II veterans who had re-acclimated to civilian pursuits. These men were called back into uniform and away from their farms, factories, businesses, and families. While reservists were rushed to the Far East, their paucity of numbers soon made it clear that a draft would be necessary.

Just over half of the American soldiers who disembarked from the *Takasago Maru* in Pusan on July 2 were age 20 or younger. They knew almost nothing about the country they would defend and the force that opposed them. The Americans' lack of training, substandard equipment, and poor physical conditioning might have been evident to some of their officers. The leadership capabilities of some commanders might also have been suspect. But no matter: only five years removed from their World War II victories, U.S. military of all ranks were imbued with the hubris that the "little yellow men" of the NKPA would recoil at the mere sight of the American flag and its uniformed soldiers.

Ignorance of Korea and the dynamic of its struggles would cost the Americans dearly.

# CHAPTER 20

# Ch'onan

By virtue of its dependence on equipment and supplies, a U.S. infantry regiment in Korea employed a fleet of trucks. Roads were at once the American Army's lifeline and its greatest vulnerability, and the North Koreans knew this.

Korean topography ensured that the roads invariably twisted around and about the lowlands between hills. Plateaus are few in South Korea, so that all the hills rise suddenly and steeply, like mounds deposited from giant dump trucks on an otherwise flat landscape. The hills are hard and rocky, and at the time featured sparse scrub pine for foliage.

Virtually all the flatlands were cultivated mostly as rice paddies, which precluded off-road vehicle travel. Roads tended to follow the contours where the steep slopes suddenly dropped to the flats. Roads that crossed rice paddies were constructed on berms. The configuration of hilltops and ridge lines provided excellent vantage points for any marksmen wishing to fire upon the roads below. Similarly, hairpin turns and switchbacks for crossing the hills were perfect places to ambush unsuspecting convoys.

Man for man, the North Korean People's Army soldier in 1950 was in better physical shape than his American counterpart yanked from occupation duty in Japan. North Korean foot soldiers readily scaled hills that would leave most Americans winded if they tried to do the same. The NKPA soldier was also necessarily resourceful. North Korean troops went to war without the support of an extensive supply network. Whereas the U.S. Army deployed up to three rear echelon troops for every American soldier "pulling a trigger," the North Korean combatant had little else supplied to him except for a rudimentary uniform. Some men, but not all, were issued weapons and ammunition. He scrounged constantly for food. While ordered to kill for ideological reasons, the NKPA soldier was often more motivated by the opportunity to obtain his victim's boots or food rations.

In the Battle of P'yongt'aek on July 6, the bloodied first battalion of the 34th Regiment lost one fourth of its original number. It withdrew through P'yongt'aek and continued south to regroup below the town of Ch'onan. Meanwhile, the regiment's third battalion, initially clustered near Ansong, also retreated to Ch'onan without having engaged the enemy at all. The NKPA did not immediately pursue because they awaited replenishment of their own ammunition; meanwhile, they delighted in collecting abandoned American provisions. On top of that, they had unanticipated numbers of prisoners with which to contend.

General Dean was furious with the 34th Regiment's disorderly withdrawal. He summarily sacked its commander, Colonel Lovless, replacing him with Colonel Robert Martin, one of Dean's former subordinates from World War II. Having just flown in from Japan, Martin arrived at Ch'onan still dressed in a class A uniform.

Ch'onan was a crossroads town, largely deserted by its residents who fled south. By the evening of July 7, the 34th Regiment had repositioned its line of resistance to the northern outskirts of town. This time, the regiment's third battalion manned the line while the first battalion bivouacked some five miles south, allowing it to recuperate from the debacle at P'yongt'aek while also protecting the southbound routes of withdrawal from Ch'onan.

For the men of Lt. Raymond Johnsen's Baker Company, a component of the first battalion, this was an opportunity to rest, replenish provisions and equipment, and compare notes about their initial combat experience.

The Americans were beginning to realize the inhospitable nature of Korean hinterlands. The soldiers' fatigue uniforms

126

began to smell of sweat and mildew. They endured the unwelcome attention of mosquitos swarming from the rice paddies. Similarly, anyone attempting a conversation often found himself spitting out flies between his words.

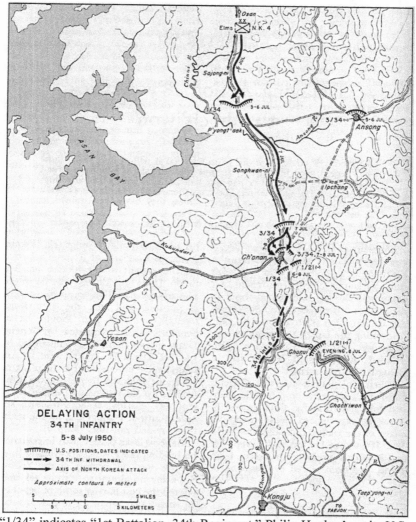

"1/34" indicates "1st Battalion, 34th Regiment," Philip Hughes's unit. *U.S. Army.*

After sunset on July 7, the NKPA advanced on Ch'onan, repeating their combined armor and infantry assault tactic. From their redoubt to the south, the first battalion witnessed the hellish nighttime scene of white phosphorus shells that illuminated the skies of Ch'onan to the defenders' advantage. The sound of artillery exchanges rumbled through the humid night air. But as the NKPA had a six to one advantage in troop strength, it was only a matter of time before the town was overrun. On the morning of July 8, Colonel Martin personally joined his men in Ch'onan to engage the enemy in combat; the cannon blast from a T-34 tank cut him in two. He had not been on the front long enough to obtain a proper outfit of combat fatigues.

Again, the Americans were routed. The mere threat of encirclement often instilled panic among the boy soldiers especially. Being surrounded meant being cut off from re-supply while losing ability to withdraw from combat if so desired. All too often, incapacitated troops were abandoned to the encroaching enemy, who thought nothing of bayonetting the prostrate and helpless. The NKPA's formula for attack would be repeated many times throughout the summer of 1950.

The stand at Ch'onan delayed the NKPA's invasion of South Korea by 14 to 20 hours. The 34th Regiment's third battalion lost 350 men in Ch'onan, two thirds of its original number. This included 60 men taken prisoner. Among the American materiel abandoned to the enemy were most of their crew-served weapons (machine guns, mortars, and recoilless rifles). Equally important was the loss of things as seemingly mundane as trailer-mounted tanks for drinking water.

Survivors continued south on foot and by truck on Saturday, July 8 to regroup on the banks of the Kum River, which provided a natural barrier in the approach to Taejon. While on their southbound march, the Americans could not help but to notice NKPA foot soldiers proceeding apace on the ridges above them. The Americans had no choice but to drink water retrieved from the rice paddies, knowing full well the nature of the contaminants suspended within. All the men would eventually suffer to varying degrees from dysentery in the coming days. Gastro-intestinal distress and bloody stool dehydrated the men and diminished their capacity to fight. Some soldiers would be hospitalized. In the worst cases, a dose of dysentery was fatal.

For their effort at Ch'onan, the 34th Regiment bought time that allowed the 24th Division to deploy additional regiments arriving from Japan, although these were also understrength and underprepared for combat. The newly-added 21st Regiment delayed the enemy's advance for three days at Choch'iwon on July 10-12, but in doing so, suffered losses greater than those sustained by the Americans at Osan, P'yongt'aek, and Ch'onan combined. General Dean would consolidate his beleaguered regiments, forming a line of resistance at the Kum River before the division's headquarters in the city of Taejon.

July 1950. Vicinity of Ch'onan, Korea. 24th Division soldiers patrol through rice paddies. *U.S. Army, Harry S. Truman Library and Museum.*

# CHAPTER 21

# The Kum River Line

I am convinced that the North Korean Army, the North Korean soldier and the status of training and the quality of his equipment have been underestimated. *Letter from Major General William F. Dean to General Douglas MacArthur, July 8, 1950*

By mid-July 1950, the U.S. 24th Infantry Division's forces in Korea were clearly overmatched. Effective resistance required more troops and supplies over and above what were already committed. The Eighth Army's commander, General Walker, knew that he had to commit to Korea the three remaining divisions performing occupation duties in Japan. The problem was that the bulk of these inputs would necessarily enter Korea through Pusan's harbor facilities, which could handle only so many ships per day.

The NKPA's advance approached General William Dean's command post in Taejon. This modest city of textile mills, tanneries, and food processing plants was normally populated by 70,000 people. The city became swollen with government and diplomatic personnel displaced from Seoul some days before. Refugees added to the number of unsettled inhabitants. There were no accommodations or food available in Taejon for the growing numbers of people displaced by war. And even if food were available, there were no means for its distribution.

Scattered throughout Taejon were the headquarters functions of the 24th Division, providing "back office" administrative, logistical, and communication support for the combat units deployed at the front. While fighting raged to the north over the previous two weeks, Taejon became increasingly packed with supply depots, maintenance facilities, and other Army logistical functions.

School yards and parks became motor pools and maintenance yards for trucks and cargo trailers. Various office buildings and stores were converted to administrative purposes. The division staff billeted in any buildings that provided adequate shelter. Crates of food and ammunition were heaped wherever space permitted. Fuel dumps required spacious lots where men pumped gasoline from large tanker trucks into rows of five-gallon jerrycans, each of which would be allotted to the division's many vehicles. Aside from jeeps and cargo trucks, there were tow trucks, ambulances, cranes, bulldozers, graders, halftracks, and tractors for pulling artillery pieces. All of these vehicles were scattered within and beyond the city limits.

Taejon was also where medical triage was conducted, the first stop for wounded troops traveling by rail to Pusan. There was even a cemetery with temporary graves for men killed in action. There were no roads that circumvented Taejon; all evacuation routes carried traffic through the city.

Taejon's defense would make strategic use of the Kum River as a natural barrier. The river's course flowed like an inverted horseshoe, from east to west around the north of the city in a large, curving arc, generally offset some ten to 15 miles from the city. At this time of year, the river's width varied between 300-400 yards, and water levels were generally low.

The 24th Division deployed two of its three regiments in a defensive line contiguous to the river: the 34th Regiment to the left (west) and the newly-arrived 19th Regiment to the north. The third regiment, the 21st, was so badly mauled over the previous days that it was deployed to the rear (southeast) of the city, where it could rest and refit. The 21st also protected the avenues of withdrawal that swung southeast from Taejon through the Sobaek mountains toward Pusan, a mere 125 air-miles away.

Arriving by truck from Ch'onan on Saturday, July 8, the 34th Regiment's first battalion established the western-most portion of the defensive line with the Kum River to their backs. Situated here, the battalion would be the first to meet the NKPA's advance. This time, the 34th Regiment was supported by the 63rd

Field Artillery Battalion's howitzers, set up across the river, two to three miles behind the infantry's line.

While bivouacked at this location, Philip's B Company received a couple batches of replacement personnel rushed over from Japan. On July 8, this included a half-dozen sergeants; on July 10 came at least 10 more non-commissioned officers and 16 privates. These however, were still not enough to restore the unit to authorized strength. No longer in contact with the enemy, the 34th Regiment dug in on hillsides that overlooked the rice paddies and road that ran between them. Morning reports would ascribe the place name "Kongju" to their location, although that village was a half mile away.

July 7, 1950. Lt. Gen. Walton H. Walker (1889-1950), left, and Maj. Gen. William F. Dean (1899-1981) confer at the airfield near Taejon. *U.S. Army, Harry S. Truman Library and Museum.*

At about the same time, the 34th Regiment received a new commanding officer to replace Colonel Martin's loss in Ch'onan. Colonel Charles E. Beauchamp, transferred in from the 7th Infantry Division, was the regiment's fourth commander since its arrival in Korea. The kind of officer who brandished a swagger stick for style, Beauchamp brought a reputation for aggressiveness, which General Dean thought would somehow compensate for the 34th Regiment's deficiencies.

The regiment would be at rest here for three full days, each dawning with dense fog that gave way to hot, muggy afternoons.

The battalion's service company was busy here, performing maintenance and restitution tasks that could not be achieved under battle conditions. Accordingly, the infantrymen could receive meals from the supply company's field kitchens, allowing them to forego the C-ration meals. For diversion, some men wrote letters to family and friends back home. Others could view the intermittent passing of cargo planes to and from Taejon's airfield. And of course, they could watch the endless flow of southbound Korean refugees – with many young men still among them – on the road below.

Philip Hughes pondered his girlfriend's photo. With each passing day, it was harder to remember her voice. How long would it take for this "police action" to run its course so he could get back to Japan? Chances were she would not wait long for him. Philip was her *onrii* companion as long as he was accessible. Philip shared the same dilemma with all the other Americans shipped to Korea. The typical Japanese girl was prepared to "butterfly" to the next available suitor when access to her current boyfriend was lacking. If she hadn't found another boy already, she was probably thinking about it. *Domo arigato.*

The American defensive line on the Kum River was set by Wednesday, July 12, but dangerously undermanned. Rifle companies were too few, and those still available remained understrength. Positions in the line were separated by gaps as wide as two miles. Communications between units remained poor at best, thanks to lost or defective equipment.

Reinforcements and materiel were delayed after July 13 in part by labor unrest at the port of Pusan. Korean stevedores conducted a sit-down strike. History is not clear about whether this was instigated by communist sympathizers or if they were simply holding out for a wage premium. Either way, this episode was to the detriment of the men holding the Kum River line.

On July 13-14, the NKPA initiated contact at various places along the river, causing some opposing American units to fall back. Other units found out too late that their positions had been surrounded by NKPA infiltrators that exploited gaps in the line, usually under the cover of darkness.

Late in the day on July 14, General Dean issued the following message to the rifle companies lining the Kum River:

> Hold everything we have until we find where we stand –
> might not be too bad – may be able to hold – make
> reconnaissance – may be able to knock these people out
> and reconsolidate. Am on my way out now.

Finding themselves under attack from the rear and on the flanks, some American units held the line longer than others, but all were eventually routed. Aware now that no quarter was given by the NKPA, the bloodied American troops became less prone to stand fast. Many men suddenly found that death or surrender were their only options. Others somehow escaped their entrapment, not by speed or stealth, but cloaked instead by the confusion of battle.

One incursion on July 14 targeted the 63rd Field Artillery positions at high noon, just as the men were lining up for chow. The enemy's attack forced the abandonment of ten howitzers and up to 80 trucks. Ninety minutes of fighting cost this unit over 130 men. The demise of the 63rd denied Lieutenant Colonel Ayres's battalion the artillery support it would need to defend the front line.

Enemy incursions compromised the defensive positions held by the 19th Infantry Regiment's rifle companies. Unit cohesion rapidly fell apart. Trucks, jeeps, and other mechanized equipment formed intermittent retreat columns on the roads cutting across the rice paddies, sometimes under fire from surrounding hills. Many vehicles and equipment were abandoned; so too were men incapacitated by wounds. If they were not left at the overrun positions, wounded were subsequently abandoned some distance into the retreat as their stretcher-born weight proved too much for exhausted comrades to bear in the searing heat.

Thirst was every man's dilemma. Trailers with potable water tanks were mostly destroyed or abandoned, while remaining trailers were road-bound and not accessible to the men traversing rice paddies on foot. The fetid, stagnant water in the rice paddies became the drink of last resort.

Some units fell back not because of the enemy's effort, but because these units suddenly found that their flanks were exposed as neighboring units had fled. Over the next few days, stragglers stumbled into Taejon, expecting to find food, shelter, and medical treatment. Then they hoped to depart via the same train station that received them earlier that month. To the soldiers routed from the Kum River line, Taejon served as a fortress, presumably a safe haven by virtue of the volume of men and activity associated with division headquarters.

As the 19th Regiment's defensive positions crumbled, Ayres again saw potential for his battalion to be enveloped by the enemy. He sought, and was granted, permission to withdraw the battalion from its advance position on the far side of the Kum River.

The trick was to disengage without the enemy's knowledge. Nighttime withdrawal from enemy contact is one of the most dangerous maneuvers that can be attempted by an infantry formation.

Waiting until dark, the battalion elements covered each other's movement, maintaining strict noise abatement discipline. Without losing a man, they maneuvered to a collection point where truck transport awaited them.

For all of Ayres's efforts, his battalion was rewarded with a new position, this time on the eastern bank of the Kapch'on River, a tributary that flowed north into the Kum. Behind them, there were no other natural barriers of consequence to aid in the defense of Taejon. His new responsibility was directly astride the road that crossed the Kapch'on as it approached Taejon from Yusong, to the northwest. This road provided the most suitable access for the NKPA's dreaded T-34 tanks, the very weapon that the Americans were least prepared to contain.

Ayres's position was tenuous at best, and the officers under his command were well aware of this. The battalion's seven hundred men, already in poor shape, were too few to resist the 2,500-strong enemy division, plus tanks, that bore down on them.

But with the collapse of the neighboring 19th Regiment, the assignment was to be shouldered entirely by the 34th.

The portion of the front assigned to Ayres's battalion was too large to be consistently fortified by the number of men available. Accordingly, Ayres positioned his manpower overlooking the bridge that the NKPA's tanks were certain to cross. There is nothing in the Korean War histories to indicate that U.S. Army engineers attempted to blow up the bridge over the Kapch'on, thus denying North Korean armor the approach to Taejon through Ayres's position.

Able and Charlie Companies formed the battalion's front line along the river to Ayres's left (west) of the bridge crossing. One platoon of Lieutenant Johnsen's Baker Company continued the line downstream (north and east) of the bridge. Ayres placed reinforcements south of the road, on slightly higher ground, behind this line. These included First Lieutenant Sam Takahara's headquarters company, to which the balance of Baker Company was adjacent to the south. Immediately behind these was Ayres's battalion command post. Beyond the 34th's position, the road to Taejon skirted the city's airstrip, then proceeded into the city itself.

General Dean originally planned to move the 24th Division out of Taejon on July 19. On the day before that, however, General Walton Walker and his pilot Mike Lynch bounced onto Taejon's airfield in his little L-5 "Sentinel" liaison aircraft. Dean met there on the airstrip with Walker, who issued the order to hold Taejon and its critical rail station for two more days – long enough for two newly-arrived divisions to pass through the ports and move up to the front line. One of these, the 1st Cavalry Division, was earmarked to relieve Dean's 24th Division. In the meantime, Dean's men had to mount their best defensive effort yet, buying time for help to arrive, but also to preserve the organizational backbone needed to survive in the meantime.

Two days. Did July 18, the day on which the order was given, count as day one? Or did Walker mean the 19th and 20th? Dean's staff didn't give it much thought until it was too late. For many of the Americans in and around Taejon, one day would become an eternity.

# CHAPTER 22

# Taejon

The Geneva Convention is an international code that attempts to civilize warfare by prescribing mutual terms of conduct for its signatories' combatants. In 1950, the United States was a signatory, but North Korea was not.

The Americans quickly became aware of the atrocities committed by the North Korean People's Army against captured soldiers. The red crosses applied to the helmets of combat medics and their ambulances were supposed to provide them some measure of protection. Instead, these symbols became targets for NKPA marksmen. Of all the Americans defending Taejon, no one knew more about what to expect from the encroaching North Koreans than the men of the 34th Infantry Regiment lining the Kapch'on River.

The NKPA could approach Taejon from any number of directions. The shallow Kum River could be easily forded, thus adding extensive river banks to the city's defensive perimeter. The 19th Regiment covered the northern approaches until July 16, when it was overrun and largely crushed, with its remnants straggling back into Taejon. This opened up the 34th Regiment's right flank, allowing the NKPA to advance, largely unimpeded, infiltrating southward and into the hills just east of Taejon. By July 19, another body of enemy troops swung west around the 34th Regiment's position, ensuring envelopment of the town from both sides.

Lieutenant Colonel Red Ayres set up his command post immediately behind the first battalion's line. His leadership experience from World War II won him a front-row seat in this conflict, one that quickly became a humiliating, dirty little scrap on behalf of a country for which he had no affinity whatsoever.

He had already lost his artillery support when the 63rd Field Artillery Battalion was overrun five days earlier. His infantry would be pitted against an enemy that was not only more numerous, but also reinforced by tanks.

July 1950. Korea. Lt. Col. Harold "Red" Ayres (1919-1989), Commander, 1st Battalion, 34th Infantry Regiment. *Combat Studies Institute, U.S. Army Command and General Staff College.*

Ayres must have been deeply troubled, but he dared not show it. Doubt is the contagious nemesis of a combat leader. He was given sacrosanct orders to hold the line, regardless of his unit's capacity to comply. Ayres had just seen his first regimental commander, Jay Lovless, sacked for withdrawing the battalion too quickly from P'yongt'aek. Then he found out that Lovless's successor, Col. Martin, lasted all of 24 hours before he was killed at Ch'onan. The bar had been set for expectations under General Dean's command.

Ayres had a career to protect. But he was preoccupied with thoughts of fulfilling his mission while minimizing the inevitable loss of the boys under his command. His thoughts must have strayed to his wife Elizabeth. Throughout Wednesday, July 19, he watched enemy forces gather a couple miles in front of him on the opposite river bank.

138

<<◇>>

The U.S. Army received some much-needed replacement soldiers in Taejon only a day or two before the 34th Regiment's anticipated showdown with the NKPA. These were more men ousted from occupation billets in Japan and sent directly to Korea on the best available conveyance. One group crossed the Tsushima Strait in the hold of a fishing boat, after which they immediately embarked northward to Taejon via train. The replacements were fewer in number than the vacancies, but even those smelling of fish were enthusiastically welcomed by the 34th's field officers. The new men were parsed out to the line companies as needed.

Among the newcomers was Sergeant Charles Leroy Stevenson, a Washington, D.C. native. If he met Philip Hughes, he would discover that their homes were separated by a 30-minute walk.

Stevenson was a seasoned veteran at age 26. He fought in Europe in the spring of 1945 then moved with his division to the Philippines just as World War II ended. By 1950, he was working in the intelligence section of MacArthur's headquarters. The Eighth Army's "Operation Flushout" apparently deemed Stevenson's work in Tokyo to be superfluous. On July 13, he wrote his mother at 224 Emerson Street, N.W. that he was being sent to Korea.

Stevenson's situation was formidable. In the span of only a couple of days, he transitioned from a desk job to carrying a rifle and commanding a combat squad in the 34th Regiment's Baker Company. The squad blended long-time company members with newcomers like himself. Stevenson would have only a few more days to reacquaint himself with combat weapons and tactics while becoming familiar with his men's capabilities. Stevenson had little more than his personality and presence to establish the legitimacy of his leadership. He did not have much time.

<<◇>>

Almost three weeks had passed since the 34th Regiment departed Camp Mower back in Kyushu. On their way to the port at Sasebo, their truck convoy passed under a railroad trestle, across which their Japanese hosts had strung up a banner announcing festivities for the upcoming Fourth of July celebration. The bold letters promised "Aerial displays, fireworks, and foot races." Fate assured that this prophesy would be fulfilled not in Sasebo, but in Korea.

Red Ayres's battalion witnessed fireworks provided by white phosphorous shells fired over Ch'onan on the night of July 7-8. The enemy's T-34 tanks instigated a relay of "foot races" from P'yongt'aek all the way to Taejon.

Now, on July 19, the prophesy of aerial displays was precipitated by clear skies. Just after 7:00 a.m., North Korean fighter planes – Soviet-built Yaks, each emblazoned with red star insignia – flew over Taejon in two groups of three. These propeller-driven planes proceeded to dive-bomb road and rail bridges on the 24th Division's avenues of withdrawal to Pusan. The Division's anti-aircraft defenses consisted of a few halftracks, each with four .50-caliber machine guns in its cargo bed. These failed to interdict these assailants. Later in the day, another flight of Yaks crossed the front lines, dropping leaflets that urged the Americans to surrender. This time, however, the crews of the defending halftracks were ready as their quad-.50 machine guns blasted two of the enemy fighters from the sky.

The U.S. Air Force rose to the challenge. At that time, the USAF was in the midst of transitioning from propeller-driven to jet aircraft. Consequently, neither type was available in great numbers during the early weeks of the Korean War. The USAF's jet fighters were based in Japan; like flying blowtorches, these fuel-hungry F-80 "Shooting Stars" had precious few minutes to maneuver in combat over Korea before they would have to break off and return to base.

Four of the F-80s tangled with an equal number of North Korean Yaks high in the sky to the west of Taejon. It was quite a show for Philip and the other infantrymen on Taejon's northwest defensive perimeter. The F-80s blasted three of the Yaks from the sky, but not before one of them crippled an F-80. The stricken

Shooting Star's pilot attempted to make a forced landing on the Taejon airstrip, but the results of this "aerial display" were fatal.

<<<>>>

All through July 19, the NKPA launched multiple troop incursions across the Kum River, including tanks. But poor communications among American units ensured that scattered sightings of the enemy were not assembled into a big picture from which command decisions could be made. Defensive units sat largely in isolation, observing the order to hold their respective positions.

As the day wore on, Ayres watched the enemy's flanking movements from his command post. It was only a matter of time before his battalion was assaulted from the front, surrounded, or both. At dusk, Ayres ordered the service company to move most of the battalion's vehicles back into Taejon; he didn't want to risk losing these assets to the enemy. He retained a couple of jeeps for runners to relay messages between his command post and the front.

The streets of Taejon had been busy throughout the day as supplies moved in from the train station and onto trucks headed to the front. Jeeps sped through at random times carrying messages between command posts that lacked reliable radio communications.

By dusk, activity in Taejon tapered off as scattered rain showers pelted the dusty city. The occasional dog scavenged the streets and alleys. Resembling a mix of German shepherd and fox terrier, these mutts were apparently a breed indigenous to Korea. Their numbers dwindled sharply after many became meals for starving civilians.

On the city's northern outskirts, the men of the 34th Regiment set up their fighting positions above the Kapch'on River. While staring across the river for signs of enemy encroachment, Philip Hughes noticed fireflies rising into the humid air of the early evening. For an instant, he interpreted the fireflies' intermittent yellow flashes as time for him to get up and go home.

Then just that quickly, Philip remembered where he was.

Troops of the North Korean People's Army communicated in the battlefield by sounding bugles and whistles. For an organization that was lacking in modern radio equipment, this was a remarkably efficient way to direct the movement of their formations, especially at night.

Around 3:00 a.m. on July 20, NKPA scouts and patrols probed the line manned by Ayres's battalion. Their cacophony of signals not only provided a sonic pathway for the main body of troops that followed, but also unnerved the defending Americans straining to see anything in the darkness before them.

Lt. Raymond Johnsen realized that his Baker Company would bear the brunt of the NKPA's attack on the first battalion's Kapch'on River position. Johnsen systematically dashed back and forth along the company's line, positioning his men and issuing words of encouragement.

The NKPA advanced in human waves that loomed suddenly out of the darkness. Not all enemy troops carried weapons. Most had a rifle, while a few others carried Russian-made burp guns, a compact, rapid-fire instrument that made a distinctive ripping sound when operated. Opposing sides would exchange fire, but this was not enough to halt the NKPA's approach. The enemy pressed his advantage by maintaining momentum, moving over and then beyond the American troops. No matter if any of the NKPA's first rank failed to neutralize an American defender; plenty of troops in the succeeding ranks would have the chance to do the same. If shot down, the enemy soldier was immediately replaced by the comrade immediately behind him.

Contact with the enemy begat hand-to-hand combat. Rifle fire was ineffective – or even detrimental – to an infantryman surrounded by enemy troops. Even if aimed properly in the dark, an M1 rifle was powerful enough at close range to send a bullet through an enemy and into a friendly soldier on the opposite side. In close quarters, the butt end of the rifle became a club or hammer in the infantryman's hands. A bayonet attached to its barrel transformed the rifle into a spear. A clenched fist, rock, a bottle, or virtually any solid object was a makeshift weapon for the soldier in close combat. So too was the infantryman's entrenching tool, or shovel, as was a knife or even the rim of his steel helmet. Men who knew how to incapacitate others with their bare hands had a ruthless advantage.

To survive this encounter, the soldier must simultaneously ascertain and neutralize the strengths and abilities of his attacker. Success in hand-to-hand combat is predicated both on skill and luck. The experience is life-altering, irrevocably burned into the memories of the men who survive it.

It is one thing for a soldier to encounter projectiles fired by a machine gun or an artillery piece over a half mile away. While certainly terrifying, there is an intrinsic fatalism in preparing for the randomness of such threats. But it is quite different for the soldier to make personal contact with his enemy counterpart – a living, breathing, kinetically charged individual who in that moment is devoid of reason and has no purpose other than to kill.

During the wee hours of July 20, 1950, at the dawn of the push-button nuclear age, this was the vicious and primitive nature of combat fought by Philip Hughes and his colleagues in the rain and mud overlooking the Kapch'on River on the outskirts of Taejon, Korea. Through sheer force of numbers, the NKPA slowly and inexorably overran first battalion's position.

When a position is overrun, it does not mean that the defenders are entirely killed or chased away. Nor is it true that the position has totally capitulated. Parts of it may stand firm, attributable to stout defense by a squad or platoon. Any "boundary" between enemy versus friendly landscape remains indistinct and fluid, fluctuating through the course of a battle.

Under Johnsen's leadership, Baker Company held its ground long enough to allow most of the first battalion to extract itself from the NKPA's path. But as the enemy onslaught ensued, even Baker Company's resistance began to falter. The company lost many men in this action, and it would be weeks before a definitive accounting of their number was achieved.

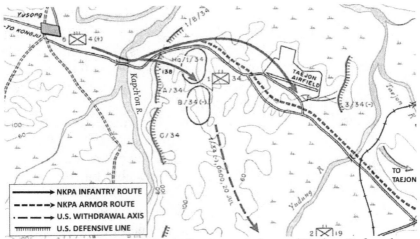

NKPA INFANTRY ROUTE
NKPA ARMOR ROUTE
U.S. WITHDRAWAL AXIS
U.S. DEFENSIVE LINE

July 20, 1950. U.S. 34th Infantry Regiment defense of Taejon. Before dawn, one arm of NKPA infantry crashed through the front line in a direct assault on 1/34's command post, shattering the headquarters company and routing Philip Hughes's Baker company in the process. Survivors of the 34th fled southward on foot, comingled with men from other units. *U.S. Army.*

<<◇>>

Enemy incursion now directly threatened Ayres's command post. He issued a last radio message back to regimental headquarters: *Tanks have penetrated my position and are headed your way.* It was about 3:30 a.m. Not long after that, Ayres and a handful of his staff quit the command post as it came under enemy fire. They had to abandon the radio jeep, thereby losing contact with the regimental switchboard.

Bullets now snapped through the air. With pistols drawn, Ayres and his staff cut a path perpendicular to the flow of NKPA troops headed southeast toward Taejon, their objective. Other American troops from the line companies, moving singly or in small groups, attempted to do the same. Only some were successful. The rest remained, either dead or incapacitated, at the defensive positions that they were ordered to hold.

By 7:00 a.m., Ayres could muster about 200 of the approximately 540 men of the 34th Regiment's first battalion. He would soon learn that his headquarters company lost one out of every three men as it bore the brunt of the NKPA attack. His line

144

companies - Able, Baker, and Charlie – sustained heavy losses as they were pushed aside. American casualty numbers would have been worse had the enemy attempted to secure the positions that they overran. There were others for whom Ayres had yet to account, as many of his men were scattered about without unit cohesion.

He led his group southward though a valley west of Taejon. Exhausted from the previous night's battle, many of the men who had not already done so would soon shed their rifles, helmets, and other equipment. Without vehicles to carry them, the weapons were burdensome weights, doubly useless if their ammunition could not be replenished.

The morning light revealed enemy movement around them. Tanks maneuvered in the flats between Ayres's position and the city, while NKPA foot soldiers closed in on the city from both the north and the west. It was clear that Taejon was no longer a safe haven. Relief would be found farther south in the direction of Pusan. The Americans would have to choose their routes carefully across the rice paddies and rolling terrain to avoid contact with the enemy.

The day was already becoming another scorcher. After wading across the Yudong River and ascending a hill south of Taejon, Ayres paused with a team of officers. From high ground just southwest of the city, they watched a calamity unfolding.

The 24th Division's rear echelon soldiers had a vague understanding of General Walker's expectation that Taejon would be held for two days, after which the division would systematically withdraw. They carried on their routine tasks, implicitly trusting the officers and infantrymen who held the defensive line at the Kum River.

Prior to the NKPA's attack, the various support soldiers were billeted in one- and two-story buildings facing directly onto the narrow streets of Taejon. Troops could see and hear what was happening to either end of their block, but no more. Over the previous days, they became accustomed to the noise of trucks and jeeps grinding their gears, mixed with the occasional clatter of tracked vehicles. So during the early morning hours of July 20, when the enemy's T-34 tanks entered the city from various directions, singly or in pairs, few men noticed. But then few of these men would have recognized a T-34 even in broad daylight.

The tanks began snaking toward the city center. They moved before headquarters troops were aware and could organize a practical resistance. One tank found a motor pool, where it promptly blew up a fuel truck. Two others surprised a kitchen unit deployed in a school yard, scattering over 150 men gathering for breakfast. Another tank targeted a medical aid station, blowing up a couple of jeeps bearing wounded men brought back from the front. The tanks began moving toward the target-rich environment that was Taejon's rail yard.

By this date, a few of the new 3.5-inch "super" bazookas had been rushed to Korea for use by the 24th Division. Weighing a mere 12 pounds, it fired a shaped charge that could penetrate up to eleven inches of armor plating, even when fired from distances of up to 900 yards. The hull of a T-34 tank was no match for this weapon. Throughout the morning, teams of U.S. soldiers unpacked and assembled the super-bazookas, anticipating an on-the-job training opportunity. They blew up at least eight tanks, while artillery men accounted for a couple more with their howitzers. This effort, however, would not save Taejon.

The city was already heavily infiltrated by enemy foot soldiers. Robed in white to mimic the civilians, troops of the North Korean People's Army entered the city clandestinely, blended with streams of refugees. These men stationed themselves throughout Taejon, first as pathfinders for the tanks, then as snipers to disrupt the Americans' defense and interdict their withdrawal.

American command communications in Taejon were almost completely compromised by defective or destroyed radios. Runners, even when dispatched by jeeps with armed guards, very often disappeared without a trace. Leadership staff did not know that much of the defensive line at the Kum River had been overrun the night before.

Having worked without sufficient sleep over the previous weeks, General Dean and his subordinate commanders began making decisions that, in retrospect, were questionable. Rather than manning his command post at the very top of the 24th Division, Dean elected to hunt tanks with a bazooka team.

Top commanders began leaving their posts. Colonel Beauchamp, head of the 34th Regiment, ventured toward the front, trying unsuccessfully to re-establish contact with Ayres's battalion. Instead, he encountered NKPA troops as his small entourage barely escaped death.

The absence or distraction of command leadership could not have come at a worse time. Without orders or effective communications, the various headquarters components could not rally an effective defense or an orderly withdrawal.

Absent any knowledge of the front line's status, most of the 24th Division assumed that the order to hold Taejon was still in effect for another day. Traffic continued arriving from the south on the morning of July 20, including a truck loaded with mail. The rail yards remained busy. Boxcars of ammunition awaited transshipment, while coaches were to be filled with stretchers of wounded returning to Pusan. The small number of troops policing the railyard were insufficient to counter the infiltrating NKPA's rifle fire. American troops had to stand guard over the locomotives' South Korean engineers – to protect them from the NKPA while also ensuring that they would not prematurely reverse away from the station.

By early afternoon, sniper fire was effectively dislodging American headquarters troops throughout Taejon. Regardless of contrary orders, various units began to pack up and withdraw. This meant loading up trucks. The Americans would carry what they could while burning or blowing up the rest. Taejon was racked throughout the afternoon by explosions, with clouds of black smoke billowing up into the hot, humid air.

In the rail yard, a locomotive engineer tied open his steam whistle, emitting a howl heard throughout the city. Noise, confusion, and panic escalated in unison.

The 24th Division formed a discontinuous caravan of over 140 vehicles to withdraw from Taejon. Two roads, plus the railroad, provided exits south toward Pusan. Given the infiltration of NKPA troops around the city, the status of these roads was uncertain.

Once underway on Taejon's cramped streets, the vehicles came under fire. Enemy snipers chose strategic targets; by picking off the driver of a lead vehicle, the resulting crash could instantly barricade the traffic behind it for a whole block. Snipers fired from rooftop positions on the vehicles attempting to reverse course on the narrow streets below. Vehicles with trailers became huge liabilities. Men disembarked from vehicles to return fire; some groups blasted through while others could not.

July 20, 1950. Taejon, Korea. 24th Division troops attempt to fight their way out of an enemy entrapment. *U.S. Army, Harry S. Truman Library and Museum.*

Columns began to disintegrate and reform as drivers branched off onto other streets, hoping to circumvent roadblocks. The enemy set up street barricades of wrecked vehicles or downed telephone poles. From these obstructions, they added machine gun fire.

Many segments of the column encountered dead-ends; the men from these vehicles had to continue on foot to the outskirts of the city and into the hills beyond, firing back at the enemy at various points along the way. Some segments of the column escaped Taejon and followed the road into the hills south of the city, only to encounter a gauntlet of fire from enemy troops perched on the hilltops above.

By dusk, the NKPA had effectively cut off routes of withdrawal for road-bound vehicles. A handful of American troops dodged the enemy while sneaking into Taejon's rail yard, seeking to commandeer a locomotive. While some of these men were without helmets or weapons, at least one of them was familiar with steam motive power operation. Luckily, they found an engine with its boiler on stand-by. Shot up and leaking steam from its ruptured boiler seams, this locomotive successfully traversed the southbound rail line, its operators tooting the whistle as it reached friendly territory by about 8:00 p.m.

This locomotive was the last vehicle to leave Taejon.

Many Americans remained trapped in the city. Ambulance drivers drove in circles searching in vain for a clear avenue of exit. Troops who were armed fought until their ammunition was expended. Many remained on foot, dashing among buildings seeking cover. The enemy torched these structures. Very few prisoners were taken. After darkness fell, fires in the city of Taejon caused the sky to glow red beneath the dense overcast.

September 30, 1950. Taejon, Korea. View upon the city's recapture by U.S. forces. *http://peacehistory-usfp.org/korean-war/*

# CHAPTER 23

# Stragglers

The U.S. Army lost almost a third of the 11,400 men committed in and around Taejon in July 1950. Among the losses was General William Dean, the 24th Division commander, who escaped Taejon and stumbled alone through the countryside for 36 days before his capture by the North Koreans. Equally crippling was the loss of cohesion and readiness, rendering the division ineffective as a combat unit. The division was forced to regroup while still on the run before an advancing enemy.

The surviving infantrymen of the 34th Regiment's first battalion were not an army, but a mob of men intermixed with little regard to unit organization. Everyone was hungry and rations were scarce. So too was water, and few if any men had purification tablets for their canteens. Cut off from their supplies, they lacked both the will and the means to fight.

It is this group that probably counted Philip Hughes among its number.

Given the North Korean's advance, the front line shifted southward accordingly. On the rail line south from Taejon, Yongdong was the first safe haven, followed by Taegu, then ultimately Pusan. Getting to friendly territory meant proceeding on foot through the hills below Taejon, hopefully evading enemy infiltrators seeking to block their way.

July 20 remained humid into the late afternoon and evening. The stragglers moved into the night. Groups of men were forced to rest at various times, too exhausted to carry on. While some of these groups caught up later, others would disappear without a trace.

<<◇>>

Officers and NCOs are responsible for the well-being of the men under their command. This involves ongoing monitoring of the men's health and morale. Sergeants especially impart the "tough love" of discipline and encouragement. This manages the troops' mood and expectations, while providing commanders with a sense of the men's capacity to function, indicating what can or cannot be asked of them.

Leadership dynamics can be damaged under extraordinary circumstances. Throughout the rout from Taejon, some officers were too exhausted, unprepared, or overwhelmed to perform leadership functions. They effectively demoted themselves and fell in with the enlisted men. Some officers did just the opposite, taking the initiative to rally the troops' focus. Both confidence and panic can be contagious; the quality of leadership decided which would prevail.

Strategies for escape varied throughout the group. Some components broke away from the main body, opting to head directly for Yongdong. The main body of stragglers was led by officers who chose to approach Pusan by heading due south of their position, then swinging eastward. But these decisions were made with imperfect knowledge of the enemy's whereabouts.

Any route taken by the battalion would be arduous. South-central Korea featured rocky hills with a growth of short, scrubby pine, indicative of a forest trying to replenish itself after decades of logging that served Japan's war needs. Treading up and down shadeless hills in temperatures at or above 100 degrees was cause for heat stroke, or at least throbbing headaches. Creeks encountered in the elevated terrain were welcome, as the water quality was preferable to what was available in the cultivated flats.

Mostly skirting roads and villages, the men entered true wilderness, where the fauna included delicate water deer that stood no more than two feet tall at the shoulder. Indigenous hare could be spotted on occasion. If the men with rifles attempted to hunt these animals, it was at the risk revealing their presence to any enemy in the area.

2001. Near Taejon, South Korea. Korean water deer. *Photo by Jinsuk Kim*

Foraging for edible vegetation yielded little satisfaction. The men found a tasteless wild fruit much like the salmon berries that inhabit the Pacific Northwest. Excursion into a rarely encountered settlement led to the discovery of a watermelon patch. The men took immediate advantage of this. The only other available food was the rations carried by a few men; these were shared among them.

After four days of moving at a snail's pace, the Americans had covered about 60 miles. A pair of young officers, Captain Sidney Marks and Lieutenant Bill Caldwell, both in superior physical condition, set out ahead of the group to reconnoiter possible resources and assistance. A day later, they found an actively-manned ROK (South Korean Army) general's command post located on a rail line. From there, the two American officers placed a call to Eighth Army headquarters:

*We've got a couple hundred men stranded at an ROK CP. How about sending up a few deuce-and-a-half trucks?*

The incredible response was that no help was available. Marks and Caldwell then negotiated with the South Koreans. At first, they made no headway with the ROKs; it's possible that the general was looking for a bribe. Marks suggested to the general that his failure to act could spark an international incident. This turned the tables. The general conceded to providing a few trucks, enough to start relaying the stragglers down to the ROK command post in stages.

At the command post, the stragglers were gathered in a schoolhouse, where they were fed with the best food available: rice, tomatoes, and potatoes, along with eggs that were hardboiled in the firebox of a locomotive stationed on a siding of the adjacent rail line. Potable water was still not available in sufficient quantity. There were, however, dozens of cases of unrefrigerated beer on hand. One beer bottle per man, plus a small ration of rice wine saki, quenched the Americans' thirst.

On July 25, the stragglers from Taejon boarded a boxcar train that took them to Yosu, a port located on Korea's southernmost coast. There, they commandeered a steamer that took all of them to Pusan. After meeting up with an Eighth Army staff officer, the men billeted overnight in another schoolhouse before refitting with weapons and equipment. The next morning, the group embarked by truck westward back to the newly aligned front – a line that would become known as the Pusan Perimeter.

While en route to the front, one section of the 34th's convoy encountered none other than General Walton Walker, head of the Eighth Army. Seeing that many of the men were without helmets, jackets, or both, Walker did what most generals are wont to do: he barked his objections to the nearest subordinate he could corner. The respondent, in this case a young lieutenant, thought quickly and responded by pointing out other deficiencies that the general hadn't seen yet – notably that many men were also lacking boots.

Walker simply grumbled and stomped back to his jeep. He didn't retract his words, as rank provided him that privilege.

Later that night, the 34th was visited by trucks bringing a supply of fatigues, jackets, helmets, and boots.

# CHAPTER 24

# The Pusan Perimeter

The North Korean People's Army pushed the American and ROK forces into a box of territory in the southeast corner of Korea. This area was bordered on the south and east by the Sea of Japan. The western and northern edges of the box became the front line against the advancing North Koreans. Much of the interior boundary, some 140 miles in all, aligned with the natural barrier offered by the Naktong River. This line – the Pusan Perimeter – delineated the last practical margin of defense for the city of Pusan and its critical port facilities. In late July 1950, the American forces anticipated subsequent withdrawal across the Naktong River into fortifications along the river's opposite bank.

The perimeter defined the "Alamo" of the Korean War.

Instead of presenting a continuous line, the Pusan Perimeter was a series of strong points. Rail and road networks behind the lines allowed the Americans to shuttle men and assets as needed, bolstering the perimeter in response to enemy incursion. Infantry, armor, artillery, and air power could be coordinated with increasing efficiency. The growing magnitude of forces deployed, plus the advent of a smaller, relatively well-defined defensive frontier would work to the Americans' advantage.

By now the 24th Infantry Division was no longer the sole American ground force committed in Korea. The 1st Cavalry and 25th Infantry Divisions were recently added to the mix, with the Marines' 1st Provisional Brigade only days away. These units would solidify the resistance maintained so far and at great cost by the 24th Division and the Republic of Korea's own indigenous army.

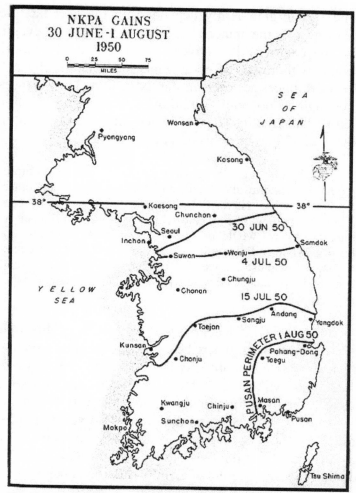

The Pusan Perimeter. *U.S. Naval Historical Center.*

There were political trade-offs as well. The United Nations as a forum condemned North Korea's aggression, yet individual member nations were slow to commit armed forces and material support to South Korea's defense. American troops hung on not only to defend a nation, but to bolster would-be allies' confidence that their contributions to the defense of South Korea had real potential for success.

The U.S. Eighth Army depended on the port facilities at Pusan to absorb the materiel needed to resist and eventually repulse the enemy. Alternatively, the port would support the systematic withdrawal of combatants, complicated by a large number of refugees seeking similar extraction. The port was not large enough to do both. Withdrawal was not just politically shameful. This reality was reflected in General Walton H. Walker's July 29 order to his division commanders:

> We are fighting a battle against time. There will be no more retreating, withdrawal or readjustment of the lines or any other term you choose. There is no line behind us to which we can retreat....There will be no Dunkirk, there will be no Bataan. A retreat to Pusan would be one of the greatest butcheries in history. We must fight until the end....We will fight as a team. If some of us must die, we will die fighting together....I want everybody to understand we are going to hold this line. We are going to win.

Walton Walker's leadership style motivated his frequent visits to the front lines, where he could see – and be seen by – the troops under his command. As the Pusan Perimeter was being fortified, pilot Mike Lynch took the general up in a series of flights over the front lines in his L-5 light aircraft. When directly over the troops, at little more than tree-top level, Lynch would throttle the plane's engine back to idle. Walker then leaned out of the open passenger door with a bullhorn in hand, issuing a mix of admonitions and encouragement to the troops below.

A precious few replacement troops filtered down to the 34th Infantry Regiment on July 23, now reforming in the vicinity of Yongdong. The newcomers' initiation to Korea involved a jarring truck ride from Pusan into the rugged countryside on roads clogged with military vehicles and civilian refugees.

Upon arrival at the 34th's encampment, the clean, fresh-faced replacements hopped off the back of their trucks, each man fully outfitted with weapons and packs of field gear. Welcomed by one of the regiment's remaining headquarters staff, the men were lined up and summarily assigned to rifle companies. Then they met face-to-face with the gaunt and tattered veterans of Taejon and the preceding battles of July. If the newcomers were anxious to know what awaited them, most veterans were equally anxious to not talk about it.

Among the replacements reaching the 34th Regiment were a couple of black soldiers. Although President Harry Truman's July 1948 Executive Order 9981 officially heralded the desegregation of U.S. armed forces, actual implementation was lagging. This was due in large part to the very top Pentagon brass who remained beholden to the sentiments of Dixiecrat legislators. Further down the chain of command, the field officers who risked their lives daily in the morass of Korea began to welcome capable soldiers regardless of ethnicity. These men would be distributed across regimental companies according only to the criterion of need. On the battlefield, at least, American soldiers of all races would share equally in the filth, deprivation, and horrors of combat.

<<<>>>

The 24th Division at the end of July 1950 was hardly combat ready. It needed to receive and assimilate its new men while allowing veterans to rest and rehabilitate. On both of these counts, the division faltered due to wartime conditions.

The North Korean People's Army continued to press southeast from Taejon toward Pusan, while also encroaching from the west, at Chinju, and along Korea's eastern coast toward P'ohang. American units newly arrived in Korea moved to the front, allowing the battered 24th Division time to catch its breath, if not fully rejuvenate. The Eighth Army assigned Major General John Church to lead the division, replacing General Dean, who was still missing in action from Taejon.

After receiving a series of tentative marching orders, Colonel Beauchamp's 34th Regiment bivouacked near Koch'ang, a settlement still in advance of the Naktong River and the Pusan Perimeter's western frontier. Here, the 34th regrouped, even as stragglers from Taejon would trickle out of the mountains for days to come. Roll calls revealed a demoralizing number of missing comrades.

The regiment had no communications switchboard, and only a handful of field radios. It had lost most of its mortars, bazookas, and machine guns. Many vehicles were destroyed or abandoned in Taejon, including too many trailer-borne tanks for potable water. This reinforced the troops' dependence on local water supplies. While the Eighth Army's transport companies continued to serve as a life-line for new equipment, the loss of vehicles organic to the regiment reduced its tactical mobility.

To haul its prodigious daily requirements of ammunition and rations, the Army often commandeered native oxen, when these were available. These draft animals were particularly useful in scaling the many slopes that were inaccessible to motor vehicles.

Another solution was offered by the civilian population still resident in Koch'ang. Regimental headquarters staff established a payroll for laborers equipped with little more than empty pockets and strong backs. Each of these men – virtually all of them too old for South Korea's military draft – came equipped with their own primitive yet ingenious backpack frame shaped like the letter "A." Known to the Americans affectionately as a "chiggie," the bearer could load and move an astonishing volume of goods on his A-frame. The daily consumables of war were distributed this way from regimental levels down through companies and platoons.

But while seeking safe harbor in Koch'ang, the Americans found a number of men, women, and children that had been executed while bound hand and foot. The police chief claimed that this was the work of North Korean infiltrators. Some civilians, however, implicated the police chief, accusing him of overzealous purging of "suspected communist sympathizers." This was not a unique incident in South Korea in 1950. Korean roads were flooded with refugees for good reason.

To American observers, Korean "friends" were physically indistinguishable from Korean "foes." The NKPA and their political operatives took full advantage of this confusion. On numerous occasions, an American soldier would march past a white-clad farmer tending a rice paddy one afternoon, only to see the same individual bearing down on him the next morning as part of an enemy attack formation.

More than one American began to question the integrity of the cause for which he risked his life.

<<<>>>

Not yet positioned behind the Naktong River, the 34th Regiment had to rest with one eye open. Regular NKPA forces were known to be in the vicinity, some of them moving south around the 34th in a flanking motion. Third battalion formed the regimental front line, while Baker Company and the rest of the first battalion deployed to the rear, covering a tree-lined stretch of road that would be the bug-out route for the 34th, if necessary.

The NKPA's inevitable advance on Koch'ang began in the pre-dawn hours of Saturday, July 29, once again precipitating the Americans' humiliating withdrawal under fire. Third battalion lost over a platoon's worth of men partly because they had no artillery support. Over the next three days, the 34th Regiment's two battalions would leap frog each other – one digging in to face enemy encroachment while the other covered the withdrawal route toward the Naktong River. The number of trucks on hand was sufficient to carry only one battalion at a time. Accordingly, the battalions took turns either riding or marching as they conducted their retreats.

Officers of the 34th Regiment, from Colonel Beauchamp on down, were well aware of the insufficient number and poor condition of their troops. Compliance with General Walker's "stand or die" order would require creativity, resourceful thinking, and a bit of stalling.

This was evident on Sunday, July 30, which dawned under a grey overcast. It was first battalion's turn to man the defensive line, this time near Kwanbin-ni. Baker and Charlie Companies dug in among the scrubby foliage on the top of small hills that overlooked a valley. Able Company was deployed forward of these hills, covering a fork in road that was the NKPA's probable avenue of approach. By dispersing its meager forces, the 34th

Regiment hoped to fool the enemy into believing that the Americans were more numerous than they actually were.

As the NKPA encroached, the Americans were supposed to pull back in ranks that covered each other's withdrawal. It didn't take much to encourage the infantrymen to disengage. They all knew by now that incapacitation in battle could result in being left to the mercy of the NKPA, a fate to be avoided at all costs.

Rain fell intermittently through the morning. The Americans knew the NKPA were approaching Kwanbin-ni when Baker Company began taking sniper fire from across the valley. But even as this transpired, at about 10:00 a.m., battalion commander Ayres took the time to enthusiastically greet another batch of replacements, this time 75 officers and enlisted men. Within ten minutes, the new arrivals were parceled out to their rifle company assignments.

The NKPA began their advance at noon, two battalions strong with more in reserve. But by 2:00 p.m., even with replacements being added, Able Company's resistance faltered as they began to suffer casualties. It pulled back to Baker Company's position, then both fell back to the battalion collection point. There, Lieutenant Chaphe, the regimental chaplain, partnered with Ayres to direct the loading of wounded men onto the available trucks for evacuation. Among the weapons left behind by the retreating Americans was a .30 caliber machine gun that the NKPA promptly turned and fired on the retreating troops.

It was all in a day's work for the boys in Korea at the end of July 1950.

War inevitably depletes a soldier's emotional reserves. The Eighth Army's harrowing experience in Korea enervated many of its men to the point of madness. Prolonged episodes of fear and anxiety, filtered through cycles of acute exposure to combat, can incapacitate man.

"Battle fatigue" describes a host of maladies that are evident in a soldier's behavioral disorganization. One indicator is the dazed facial expression known as the thousand-yard stare. The soldier may also display slower reaction times, an inability to prioritize tasks, and an apparent disconnection from his immediate surroundings. In short, battle fatigue renders him useless as a fighting man.

The remedy involves at least removing the man from combat for a period of time. While each soldier has a limit to his tolerance, neither training nor pre-selection can effectively preclude the onset of battle fatigue. Tolerances can be made somewhat elastic by employing a sense of humor. Troops also find some relief by singing in cadence with their marching.

Fortuitous timing allowed the Americans in Korea to co-opt a contemporary tune by the Canadian singer Hank Snow. "I'm Movin' On" was ostensibly a truck driver's lament rendered with a country swing. The song in its entirety was as innocent as its first verse:

> *That big eight-wheeler rollin' down the track*
> *Means your true-lovin' daddy ain't comin' back*
> *'Cause I'm movin' on, I'll soon be gone*
> *You were flyin' too high, for my little old sky*
> *So I'm movin' on*

"I'm Movin' On" made its way onto Armed Forces Radio Network broadcasts. It was probably assimilated by drivers of the Eighth Army's transport companies, who in turn shared it with men all through the combat supply chain, from the port in Pusan to the front lines. Soldiers took the liberty of modifying the lyrics to suit their circumstances. Ruminating on the dreaded strategy of delay and retreat, "Bug-Out Boogie" emerged as the unofficial anthem of fighting men in Korea.

The lyrics morphed over time as the Americans fought through the summer and fall of 1950. Immediately cynical and ribald, the modified lyrics unequivocally captured the American soldier's Korean War experience. One rendition of the song began as follows:

*Hear the patter of running feet*
*It's the old First Cav in full retreat*
*They're moving on; they'll soon be gone*
*They're haulin' ass, not savin' gas*
*They'll soon be gone.*

That opening verse was typically modified to implicate the singer's neighboring organization. By the end of 1950, the lyrics reflected China's commitment to the fray:

*Over on that hill there's a Russian tank*
*A million Chinks are on my flank*
*I'm movin' on, I'll soon be gone*
*With my M1 broke, it ain't no joke*
*I'll soon be gone.*

*Million Chinks comin' through the pass*
*Playin' burp-gun boogie all over my ass*
*I'm movin' on, I'll soon be gone*
*With my M1 broke, it ain't no joke*
*I'll soon be gone.*

*Twenty thousand Chinks comin' through the pass*
*I'm tellin' you, baby, I'm haulin' ass*
*I'm moving on; I'll soon be gone*
*I'm haulin' ass, not savin' gas*
*I'll soon be gone.*

*Standin' in a rice paddy up to my belly*
*From then on, they called me "Smelly"*
*I'm moving on; I'll soon be gone*
*I'm haulin' ass, not savin' gas*
*I'll soon be gone.*

*Here's papasan comin' down the track*
*Old A-frame strapped to his back*
*He's moving on; he'll soon be gone*
*He's haulin' ass, not savin' gas*
*He'll soon be gone.*

*Here's mamasan comin' down the track*
*Titty hangin' out, baby on her back*
*She's moving on; she'll soon be gone*
*From her tits to her toes, she's damn near froze*
*She'll soon be gone.*

*I sung this song for the very last time*
*Gonna get Korea off my mind*
*I'm moving on; I'll soon be gone*
*I done my time in the shit and slime*
*I'm movin' on.*

On August 1, General Walker ordered all Eighth Army elements across the Naktong River. Crossing on the next day, the 34th Infantry Regiment approached its next encampment, another collection of thatched-roof wattle huts, this one being the village of Yongsan. For now, the 515 men of the 34th's first battalion would be placed in reserve, while the third Battalion's 493 men manned their portion of the Pusan Perimeter.

As the NKPA increasingly conquered South Korea, even more refugees took to the roads. Heading generally for Pusan, most of their numbers bottlenecked at the Naktong's few bridge crossings. Anticipating the Eighth Army's complete deployment on the east bank of the river after August 2, American combat engineers rigged these bridges for demolition, intending to destroy the spans as soon as all their troops and assets crossed. This task was frustrated by hordes of refugees also seeking to cross the river.

On the bridge near Wigwam, in the 1st Cavalry sector, the engineers tried to prevent refugees from crossing. Several attempts to block them failed, as the civilians stayed literally on the heels of the retreating army. With the NKPA closing in, division headquarters gave the order to blow the bridge. The refugees would not vacate the bridge, despite all manner of warnings. Did this indicate their depth of fear of the NKPA forces, or was it a simple misunderstanding? When the combat engineers pushed the detonation plungers, the hundreds of refugees who perished on this one bridge took the answer with them to their deaths.

1950. South Korea. American troops perched on an M39 tracked utility vehicle watch as a young Korean woman carries a small child in search of a place where they can survive another day. *pinterest.com*

# CHAPTER 25

# Boys at War

Philip Hughes was exhausted at the end of July 1950. He had been on the run for the better part of a year since he and Frank slipped out of the cottage at Rehoboth Beach. The peacetime Army promised an idyllic escape that all too suddenly turned into a nightmare.

He found himself in a remote corner of Asia with its foul and inescapable odors, bugs, and scorching summer heat. Even when he wasn't engaged in battle, Philip was haunted by what he had endured, and anxious about what was to come. The Army was no longer a game.

Philip, like all the other Americans, was largely unprepared for a war he did not expect to fight. He went to Korea outfitted in a uniform and with equipment designed for World War II specifications. He was weighed down with belts, pouches, bags, a knife, tenting hardware, and rolled bedding. His "steel pot" helmet weighed just under three pounds. He may have been tempted to discard his helmet, as so many other soldiers did during July, due to its cumbersome fit and the oppressive summer heat. And like the other men, he would untuck his tunic to gain slight relief from the heat and insects.

Aside from his rifle, Philip carried ammunition in a quantity that traded off his killing capacity for personal mobility. The M1 rifle required clips of eight rounds (cartridges) per clip. Philip wore a canvas cartridge belt with up to ten of these clips along with three hand grenades. Other paraphernalia, aside from the weapons, became superfluous in the summer of 1950, when heat and unreliable transportation took a toll on soldiers in the field. A staggering volume of gear littered Korean roadsides after American units rushed to stay ahead of the advancing enemy.

Like most of the Army's lowest-ranking soldiers, Philip had no concept of his location except that he was "somewhere in Korea." He moved about the countryside every few days, either on foot or by truck, at the whim of upper command. Platoon commanders provided the men situational awareness, usually preceded by the announced intention to take yet another hill. This information was imparted to Philip and his colleagues by gathering them in a circle, where a lieutenant or sergeant drew in the dirt with a stick, depicting landscape objectives. Given the tedium of field deployment interspersed with the sporadic terror of combat, the boy soldiers longed for home more than they cared about their proximate location in Korea.

July 31, 1950. Korea. Twenty-one-year-old Jim Sullivan, 19th Infantry Regiment, from Modesto, California, keeps watch from a foxhole while his buddy sleeps. Both are armed with M1 rifles. Sullivan was due to be discharged in July 1950, but the war changed that. *U.S. Army, Harry S. Truman Library and Museum.*

Philip spent most of July 1950 living outdoors. His sleep was sporadic and elusive, for wherever he bivouacked, he took turns during the nights standing watch for perimeter security. When he could sleep, he usually did so on the ground without fixed shelter. All the soldiers learned to catch sleep in fits and starts, between tasks. On occasion, they found shelter in a farm house or outbuilding that may or may not have been abandoned by its owners. The more typical scenario involved digging a foxhole in the rocky soil. Only then could Philip surrender to exhaustion, wearing the same clothes in which he had marched around all that day, the day before, and the day before that.

The consequences of sleeping on the ground with poor sanitation were unpleasant. At some point, Philip contracted body lice, or "cooties," as some men called them. About the size of a sesame seed, the louse is an insect that feeds on the blood of its host, causing severe itching and skin irritation. Lice gather where body hair is thickest, and they lay eggs (nits) in the seams of clothing. At the time, the best practice for their eradication involved a prolonged boiling of clothes and a body spray of DDT or lindane, both of which were later determined to be carcinogenic.

Laundry and bathing facilities were sporadically available to the troops, usually when they were sufficiently removed from the front lines. Quartermasters provided replacement clothing periodically to troops on the battlefield. Given the limitations of supply logistics, soldiers could not always expect properly tailored uniforms. Ill-fitting boots were especially problematic. Frequent, extended marches often caused swollen and blistered feet.

The troops in Korea were bedeviled by flies, mosquitoes, a wide assortment of millipedes, and rodents, especially in the flat lands where agriculture was tended. Woe befell the soldier who completed a foxhole in the dark, only to find that the location was inhabited by one of the 137 species of ants native to Korea.

Mosquito netting was a premium commodity; sheets of it could be cut into swatches to be worn over the face and head. Bug repellant, distributed only when it was available, was an all-or-nothing proposition. Failure to apply it to the lips meant they would be swollen the next morning by bug bites. The boys slathered on enough bug repellant that their foxholes would often reek of it.

Exposure to these pests diminished with altitude, a fact that helped motivate men to scale the Korean hills not just for tactical advantages, but also to minimize their own nighttime discomfort.

<<<◇>>>

That "an army marches on its stomach" is an enduring truism. In peacetime conditions, Army food was plentiful, if lacking in variety and flavor. Wartime conditions further compromised the quality and quantity of food available to soldiers in the field. Hunger allowed troops to forgive the army for many of its culinary sins.

Philip, like all the other troops sent to Korea in 1950, subsisted primarily on surplus C-rations from World War II. A single C-ration was designed to feed one man for one day. The contents were enclosed in a cardboard box. Eight of these boxes were delivered in a wooden crate, each just over one cubic foot in capacity, weighing 40 pounds. Once expended, the crates often became firewood.

Upon opening the carton, the soldier found six 12-ounce cans, two for each meal of the day. A pair of cans consisted of the meal's "M" unit, featuring some combination of meat and starch, while the other, or "B" unit, contained several calorie-dense crackers, a package of sweets like Brach & Sons vanilla caramels or Jim Dandee cookies, and an instant coffee or powdered drink mix. The cans were labeled as to their contents. Once separated, the ration items could be distributed among various pockets or tucked in a musette bag – a small backpack – slung over the shoulder.

A limited variety of menu items were found in the crates of rations delivered to the front. The soldiers quickly developed preferences. A typical breakfast's "M" unit might be ham and eggs. Canned peaches were treasured because the juice was a source of clean water. Lunch or dinner selections included "beans with frankfurter chunks" or the mysteriously subtle variations of "meat and beans," "meat and vegetable stew," or "meat and vegetable hash." Even less popular were the ham and lima beans. Soldiers learned the hard way that "beef with gravy" was susceptible to spoilage if the cans were left too long in the hot sun. Then there was corned beef hash, which the men referred to derisively as "pigshit." All of the canned meat products tended to have a high fat content. Some soldiers developed heartburn if they subsisted too long on such fare.

C-rations could be eaten cold if necessary, or heated in the can. If a truck or armored vehicle was idling nearby, a soldier could effectively heat his canned ration can by placing it on the vehicle's exhaust manifold.

The C-ration carton also contained a kraft paper pack of accessories, which included sugar tablets, salt tablets to regulate fluid loss, a bottle of halazone tablets for water purification, a flat wooden spoon, chewing gum, several sheets of toilet paper, a Gillette safety razor, and a compact can opener, which the soldier would thread onto the same neck chain that held his dog tags.

1950. Korea. Chow is served on the front lines. *U.S. Army, Harry S. Truman Library and Museum.*

A resourceful company cook could assemble "chow" by pooling multiple rations into a communal cooking vat. The more enterprising cooks bartered with locals to gather poultry, swine, and assorted vegetables to supplement the monotonous C-ration fare. Soldiers learned how to incapacitate fish by tossing hand grenades into streams and ponds, thus adding to the menu. When roads permitted, truck-bound field kitchens made itinerant stops behind the front. Men would rotate from the line in shifts to collect their meal. Food serving required each man to present his mess kit, a hinged metal plate with an accompanying metal cutlery set. Care was taken to not queue up too tightly for chow, as this presented a tempting target for enemy snipers.

Sometimes, conditions dictated that hot food be carried to the front in insulated Mermite containers. The availability of hot food, however sporadic, made a material contribution to the morale of men in combat. Soldiers appreciated cooks who advanced to the line not just to serve food, but to share the risk of combat exposure.

Of all the C-ration accessories, the most prized may have been the packs of commercial-grade cigarettes accompanied by a book of 20 cardboard matches. Smoking was a detriment to the soldier's respiratory capacity (a factor when scaling Korean hills), but it also calmed the nerves. The very act of managing and using one's cigarette supply provided some distraction from the anxieties of war.

Cigarettes were also instruments of camaraderie: it was a symbolic ritual of initiation to offer a smoke to a newcomer. So too was the gesture of placing a cigarette between the lips of a man about to be carried away on a stretcher. Army cigarette rations instigated life-long nicotine habits for countless men. If Philip Hughes did not pick up a smoking habit in Japan, he almost certainly did in Korea.

Military medical officers monitored the army's health challenges peculiar to operating conditions in Korea. They found it necessary to supplement rations with several special items rushed to the battlefield for distribution. Extra salt tablets were issued. Notoriously bitter chloroquine pills were prescribed once per week to neutralize malaria-bearing parasites. Another specialty item was cheese, which gave soldiers relief from the loose bowel symptoms of dysentery.

Access to clean water was an exception rather than a rule. When deployed in combat, units organized water details – usually tasked to one man at a time, who started by collecting his colleagues' canteens. He would then dash to a nearby river or stream, where he methodically filled each canteen, then lugged the lot of them back to his unit. Water details ran all day long as the duty was rotated through the platoon roster.

Sanitation for troops in Korea was abysmal. The Army field manual prescribed the provision of latrines, a task that required digging a slit trench and installing over it a wooden board as a "user interface." Given a latrine's tendency to attract flies and rats, it was a maintenance imperative to apply lye periodically to the latrine's contents and neutralize it by lighting it on fire. But only under the best of conditions could these measures be applied.

All too often, infantry positions were tenuously held, so that the men lacked the time to properly prepare such facilities. The next alternative, then, was to designate a natural feature – a cluster of bushes or rocks – as the "place to go." Maybe the men would consistently use that place, or maybe they wouldn't. Regardless of the facilities provided, soldiers were extremely hesitant to leave their fox holes at night, lest a trigger-happy colleague mistake them for an enemy intruder. This inconvenience inspired yet another use for the soldier's helmet, if only in the most dire of emergencies.

During the first year of the Korean War, 60 percent of U.S. troop evacuations for hospital care were disease related. The rest were split between battle related injuries and non-battle incidents (traffic mishaps and other infrastructural chaos that prevailed especially during the initial stages of the war).

A wide variety of diseases incapacitated Army ranks during the summer of 1950. The most prevalent were sexually transmitted diseases, often manifested in Japan but subsequently festering among troops sent to Korea. Opportunities to contract venereal disease quickly grew in Korea itself, especially in rear areas where non-combat troops congregated.

Many illnesses were the consequence of crowded, unsanitary conditions. Infectious diseases included hepatitis, malaria, dysentery, hemorrhagic fever, tuberculosis, rheumatic fever, Japanese encephalitis, polio, scarlet fever, small pox, scrub typhus via mites, and louse-borne typhus. A variety of respiratory diseases could be contracted. "Dust pneumonia," for example, resulted from the inhalation of dry soil particulates made airborne by vehicular movement or the concussion of weapons. An afflicted soldier could blow only so much mud from his sinuses before the dust began to choke his lungs.

For his troubles, the American soldier received an extra 50 dollars per month on top of his base salary. "Combat pay," it was called.

During the years immediately prior to 1950, the U.S. Army became the employer of last resort for teenage boys who were not yet prepared to enter adulthood. Add to this the lackluster economy of the late 1940s, and Army enlistment became almost irresistible to many boys living in tenuous circumstances.

If the Army's personnel policy was a willing instrument of social stabilization, it apparently did little to ensure combat effectiveness. Seeking to replenish its combat losses during the summer of 1950, the Army's selective service criteria drafted men in their early to mid-20s – men of somewhat greater maturity and fortitude than the teenagers. But until the draftees arrived in Korea in appreciable numbers at the end of the year, the teenage soldiers from occupation duty would shoulder the burden of combat. While awaiting the influx of draftees, the Eighth Army continued to draw replacements from personnel remaining in Japan.

The war zone was merciless to newly-arrived replacements who were pitched into combat with little to no orientation. These men were trucked in at random times, day or night. Enemy insurgents operating behind American lines sometimes ambushed these trucks on their way to the front. If he successfully reached his debarkation point, the replacement soldier would then proceed on foot – probably uphill – to report to his assigned company command post. Not yet familiar with friendly versus enemy positions and fields of fire, the replacement's trek to his new combat assignment was sometimes his last.

Odds of a rifleman's survival was a frequent subject of conjecture among soldiers. It was generally evident to all that new men suffered higher casualty rates. The consensus was that a newcomer had a 75 percent chance of being hit in his first three days of combat. During the 90 days that followed, the casualty rate was deemed to be only 25 percent. Any time in combat after those 90 days boosted the casualty rate again to 75 percent due to the soldier's complacency.

The age of the American soldier's adversary in Korea varied widely. The North Korean People's Army fielded small peasant boys well under the age of 16 who marched alongside veterans of Japanese resistance fighting.

To the Americans, any one of them was derisively labeled as a "gook." But at the same time, the Americans respected their adversaries' prowess in battle. Discipline and calisthenics partially compensated for the young NKPA soldier's lack of logistical support. He had little formal education. Cultural isolation in a far corner of Asia practically guaranteed his estrangement from international (mostly European) standards for the conduct of war.

Among the ranks of NKPA soldiers were commissars, who served two purposes: to motivate soldiers through ideological indoctrination, and to enforce compliance with orders, even to the point of death. The commissar was critical to the NKPA's success in battle. Armed foot soldiers constituted the first wave of an NKPA attack. Unarmed soldiers made up a second wave, as they were expected to pick up the weapons of soldiers felled from the first wave. Commissars, armed with burp-guns, followed in the third wave, in part to fire on any of their own troops who attempted to retreat.

<<<>>>

The U.S. Eighth Army deployed a number of chaplains to Korea, distributed unevenly across its divisions and regiments. Chaplains serving combat units were typically junior officers (captains and lieutenants). They were a random mix of Protestants, Catholics, and Jews. By extending religious guidance and service, chaplains were integral to sustaining troops' morale. Korea would be the second war for most chaplains, as most of the cohort available in 1950 had been commissioned during World War II.

1950. Korea. U.S. Army troops receiving communion on the battlefield. *U.S. Army, Harry S. Truman Library and Museum.*

Chaplains were nominally assigned to the headquarters company of a regiment. But given their uneven availability, most chaplains adopted an itinerant approach, using jeeps to make the rounds among infantry, artillery, engineer, and other service units. Aside from providing worship services on Sabbaths, the chaplains counseled the men, visited the wounded, and corresponded with the families of soldiers killed in action.

International convention recognized military chaplains as non-combatants. As such, chaplains were not supposed to carry personal sidearms. During the fluid, tumultuous battles of the first year of the Korean War, chaplains often found themselves in the thick of combat. Some were captured or killed. Given the threat posed by infiltrators behind the lines, many chaplains began carrying a carbine or a pistol for their own protection.

The 34th Infantry Regiment included chaplains Elwood Temple, a Presbyterian; and Carrol Chaphe, a Methodist. Catholic representation was provided by Major Edward Dorsey, a 38-year-old Washingtonian.

Like the other chaplains, Dorsey had a foot locker containing liturgical linens, chalices, hymnals, and other tools of his vocation. When conducting Mass, the hood of his jeep served as the altar. He donned the appropriate vestment over his fatigues, ministering to men seated on the ground with rifles slung over their shoulders, not too far removed from the front lines.

There is no record of Philip Hughes attending a battlefield Mass. Estranged as he may have been from his mother and his religion, Philip must have sought spiritual relief from the stress of combat. Being well-schooled in his faith, Philip may have at least considered visiting with a Catholic chaplain to seek penance, thereby receiving absolution for past sins. What weighed on his conscience? Carnal knowledge gained out of wedlock? Perhaps it was stealing money from the collection plate as an altar boy – the vice that probably financed his runaway excursion to Chicago.

It's very possible that Philip Hughes met Major Dorsey. By coincidence, Dorsey served during the early 1940s with a Dominican order at Catholic University, in Brookland, a mere 15-minute walk from Philip's home. If they realized this connection, they may have been simply amused. Or they could have perceived it as providence.

# CHAPTER 26

# The Naktong Bulge

The Naktong River begins in the Taebaek Mountains of Korea, running mostly from north to south some 314 miles before it empties into the Sea of Japan. It drains a watershed of over 9,000 square miles. Flowing with a languid current, the Naktong twists and loops through South Korea's hilly landscape, carving out irregular flats of marshland and sand beaches. Long-necked white cranes and other birds patrol the river's many shallows for frogs, crayfish, and minnows.

For ages, Koreans have dutifully cultivated rice, barley, wheat, and rye in the Naktong valley, while the hillsides are successively terraced for growing peppers, beans, and other specialties.

Deforestation of Korea during the Japanese occupation allowed soils to erode from the hills, cumulatively silting rivers like the Naktong, which in 1950 was wide but rarely deep. The river's condition was exacerbated by drought prevailing that summer.

Clusters of hills overlooking both sides of the river are wrinkled with folds and saddles. This rugged landscape facilitated stealthy infiltration by the North Korean People's Army. Once entrenched in the hills, the NKPA increasingly threatened the Eighth Army's road-bound lines of supply and communications.

The first few days of August saw a lull in the fighting as the opposing armies regrouped after the sustained battles of July. The NKPA needed its supplies to catch up to its front line of advance. Meanwhile, the U.S. Eighth Army assimilated newly arrived units to fortify its defense of the Pusan Perimeter.

Although it desperately needed rehabilitation, the 24th Infantry Division remained on the line, joined now by seven other divisions: two American and five South Korean. Equally important was the pending arrival of another U.S. Army division plus a couple of brigades, one of U.S. Marines and the other of British Commonwealth soldiers.

Philip Hughes's 34th Regiment held responsibility for a portion of the perimeter aligned perfectly with a spot where the Naktong River curved sharply westward then back again to the east, which on the map traces a large letter "C." The land outlined by this loop measured four miles east-west and five miles north-south. History today recognizes this feature as the "Naktong Bulge." The geography of the bulge was convenient to the NKPA's goals, providing the opportunity for crossing the Naktong at a point where its exposure to American artillery was minimized.

Upon initial deployment on the perimeter, the 34th Regiment's third battalion held the line while first battalion, including Philip's Baker Company, camped in reserve near the village of Yu-ri. Here, the headquarters company set up shower facilities and provided the men with fresh clothing. Their rest would not last more than a few days.

General Walton Walker's "stand or die" order on July 29 put an end to the delay and retreat tactics. More to the point, Eighth Army units were ordered to counterattack whenever possible, as doing so would keep the enemy off-balance. All units dispatched platoon- or squad-sized patrols to monitor activity between their embedded strong points. They placed listening posts forward of their lines each night, not necessarily to engage enemy infiltrators, but to observe and report their movements.

By August, the Americans approached a parity of numbers with the NKPA. They also gained control of the skies as the U.S. Air Force finally deployed a sufficient number of aircraft in both Korea and Japan. The NKPA, however, still held the initiative. For the next six weeks, all along its 140-mile frontier, the Pusan

Perimeter would become a beehive of activity as the defenders played deadly cat-and-mouse with North Korean infiltrators seeking to divide and conquer the Eighth Army's line of resistance.

At one minute after midnight on Sunday, August 6, about 800 NKPA troops gathered on the banks of the Naktong at the site of the Ohang Ferry. Their signalmen fired series of red and yellow flares into the night sky to coordinate their river crossing. Most of them landed on the eastern bank of the bulge, while others flanked to the North to enter the hills. The enemy proceeded inland until encountering the lines of the 34th Regiment's third battalion.

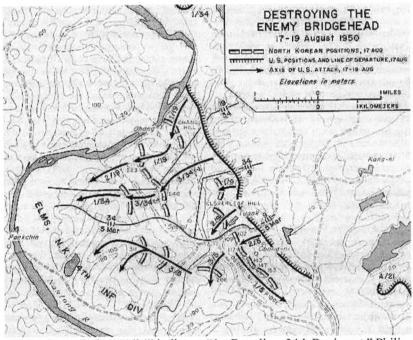

The Naktong Bulge. "1/34" indicates "1st Battalion, 34th Regiment," Philip Hughes's unit. *U.S. Army.*

It wasn't until daylight that the scale of the incursion became evident to the 34th's commander, Colonel Beauchamp. With NKPA troops advancing between and beyond strongpoints in the line, he had no choice but to call up his reserve elements. By 6:30 the following morning, Philip Hughes, Baker Company, and the rest of the first battalion were once again committed to battle, in what would become known as the "First Battle of Naktong Bulge."

There was never a single continuous battle line. In the coming days, the opposing forces would weave through the Korean hills seeking to outflank, isolate, and destroy one another. The American infantrymen secured occasional help from a precious few mechanized assets, including a couple of M-24 Chaffee light tanks and halftracks bearing quad-.50 machine guns.

In one engagement, one of the M-24s supporting Baker Company took hits from an NKPA anti-tank rifle. Philip watched as the commander of the second tank emerged from his machine and ran under fire to attach a tow chain to the stricken M-24 and pull it with its crew to safety.

The terrain itself sometimes negated the advantages of mechanized weaponry. The Battle of Naktong Bulge was a collection of clashes conducted where opposing forces met on the irregular ridge lines of Korean hills. Many slopes could only be scaled on foot. Too exhausted to charge, and armed with no more firepower than what they could carry, the combatants were sometimes reduced to tossing hand grenades over a ridgeline at opponents that were as little as ten paces away.

Close quarters allowed combatants to verbally threaten or otherwise intimidate each other, especially at night. American troops encountered the occasional North Korean who knew enough English to either hurl obscenities or to issue the unnerving taunt, *You die, G.I.!*

Curiously, the Americans and North Koreans were more likely to share a working knowledge of the Japanese language. This was useful not only in close-quarters fighting but also for the interrogation of prisoners of war.

Actual combat taught the infantryman lessons that he never anticipated in training. The North Koreans were maddeningly adept at sneaking up on their opponents at night. Many American soldiers stared into the darkness from their foxholes, only to be killed or injured by an enemy that went undetected until it was too late.

Often, a very particular design flaw of the M1 rifle was at fault. At issue was the metal clip that was used to insert eight cartridges at a time into the rifle's magazine. The rifleman pulled the trigger once per cartridge; after the eighth discharge, the M1's magazine automatically expended the metal clip, which popped into the air with an audible "ping" sound. The rifleman would then have to reach for another clip and reload his rifle, a chore that effectively disarmed him for a few seconds. For the close-in enemy stalker, the "ping" sound signaled his opportunity to strike. World War II veterans taught boy soldiers in Korea a life-saving defensive trick for nighttime combat: save an empty clip, then throw it against a rock so that the "ping" sound coaxed hidden enemies to come forward – at which time they would be dispatched accordingly.

By August 9, it was clear to Eighth Army leadership that the 34th Regiment, like the rest of the 24th Division, was largely ineffective in combat. Dysentery and dehydration still debilitated the men. There were days when the best these soldiers could do was crawl up the slopes on their hands and knees. Their inability to move, much less fight, put the rear area's lines of supply and communication at risk.

Threatened by enemy incursion, the 24th Division's command post elements began moving back, away from the fighting. Fragmentation of the command post compromised the division's ability to manage its assets and coordinate the movement of its field units. Even worse, by Saturday, August 12, the enemy had control of just under three and one-half miles of the division's main supply and casualty evacuation route.

To sustain its battle commitment, the 34th Regiment ordered its cooks, engineers, maintenance men, and even band musicians to take up arms. Still, the headcount of rifle companies and platoons remained far below authorized strength. Division headquarters somehow communicated the need for resupply of food, water, and ammunition, which was achieved by airborne parachute drops. Some of these materials landed within areas of friendly control; some did not. Plus, the drop frequently caused water containers to burst. Philip and his colleagues had no choice but to continue the details for retrieving river water.

Despite these conditions, allied elements organized a counterattack against the enemy forces holding the Naktong bulge. The U.S. Air Force now became a decisive factor. While airplanes were sighted daily high up in Korean skies, it was quite a different experience to see them provide close air support at low level. For this purpose, the air force employed single-seat fighter-bombers, which usually arrived in flights of two or four at a time. Pilots often flew low enough to pass between hills instead of over them.

Some flights consisted of F-80 jets, used increasingly for ground-attack missions because the North Korean air force by this time had been practically destroyed.

C. 1951. Korea. The F-51 Mustang fighter-bomber worked so well in World War II that the U.S. Air Force recalled it for service in Korea. Its ground support capabilities were peerless. *U.S. Air Force.*

Most air support early in the Korean War, however, came from the F-51 Mustang, a sleek propeller-driven plane built originally for World War II. The Mustangs were recalled from retirement and coaxed back to life for an encore engagement in Korea.

Philip and many other hard-pressed infantrymen cheered the arrival of the Mustangs, which made a distinctive whistling sound as they pulled out of their dives, then issued a thundering *blap-blap-blap* as their propellers cut through the air overhead. Ground troops especially appreciated the Mustangs for the menace they posed to the enemy. Their slower speed and longer endurance allowed these planes to expend their firepower with devastating accuracy.

Philip watched the air force bring formidable ordnance to the fray. The typical fighter-bomber aircraft employed six .50 caliber machine guns, while a combination of bombs and rockets were launched from beneath their wings. Perhaps the most fearsome weapons dropped by these aircraft were canisters of napalm, which split open upon impact to wash the ground with an ignited mixture of jellied gasoline. A napalm strike caused black smoke and orange flames to swirl upward together in an expansive fireball seen from miles away. When viewed through binoculars, the explosion made shock waves that visibly rippled the surrounding air. The combustion siphoned oxygen from the atmosphere. This would either asphyxiate the targeted troops, or if they were truly hapless, they would be immolated by the jelled substance that clung to everything as it burned. After the airplanes cleared the skies, Philip and the others could hear the cries of burning men. If the wind blew in their direction, they could smell the results as well.

By mid-August, the nights became noticeably chillier. The cool night air fostered a thick fog that rose from the valleys. It was mid-morning before the fog finally dissipated. It was in the pre-dawn fog of August 16 that the NKPA launched an all-or-nothing attack on American positions. Philip's Baker Company pulled back from Hill 91. Sunrise found them sloshing through marshes and rice paddies to higher ground a mile away. Fortunately, an artillery complement covered their withdrawal.

Neither side could get an upper hand in the Battle of Naktong Bulge through their intermittent sparring. The NKPA were too lightly equipped, while the Americans units were undermanned and physically spent. Frustrated by the standoff, General Walker called up the newly-arrived 1st Provisional Marine Brigade.

Like their Army counterparts, the Marines were youngsters with veteran officers and non-coms. However, the Marines trained to a more physically and mentally demanding standard than that imposed by the Army. They were also imbued with bravado derived from their well-storied exploits in the "big war." Throughout the Pacific island-hopping battles of World War II, the Marines were the vanguard of virtually every U.S. attacking force, relying on the Army for subsequent mop-up duties. In Korea, the order was reversed, with the Eighth Army holding the line from the beginning.

On Thursday, August 17, 1950, the Marines leaped from their trucks to greet the Army soldiers facing the Naktong Bulge. In the time-honored spirit of inter-service rivalry, the Marines heckled the "doggies," as they liked to call the Army men.

*You can go home now, Junior. Us men are taking over. Where the hell are the gooks?*

Philip and the other Army men, too beleaguered to take much offense, knew that if they had not held the line for the past six weeks, there would have been no place for the Marines to make their initial deployment.

By August 19, the Army and Marine combination finally out-gunned the NKPA, methodically retaking the bulge, one hill after another, until the surviving enemy was forced back across the Naktong River. Although on the side of victory, the entire 24th Infantry Division was so debilitated that it was more of a liability than an asset on the field.

On August 20, General Walker ordered the newly-arrived 2nd Division to relieve the 24th. Over the course of a couple of days, the entire 24th Division was summarily trucked to Kyongsan, where a rest camp was established well behind the battle lines of the Pusan Perimeter. The 24th completed 55 days of combat.

# CHAPTER 27

# Easy Sailing

Kyongsan was perhaps 50 miles to the northeast, as the crow flies, from the Naktong Bulge. To make the trip, Philip Hughes and his colleagues scrambled aboard the cargo beds of the regiment's GMC deuce-and-a-half (2½-ton capacity) trucks. Each truck typically held ten fully-equipped infantrymen, seated on fold-up benches on either side of the cargo bed. In a pinch, with the cargo deck's gate down, one or two more men could perch on the trailing edge with their legs dangling off the rear. Canvas covers for the cargo beds were removed due to the summer heat.

Noise added to the motoring experience. Like many military vehicles without mufflers, the GMC trucks alternately growled and whined as drivers shifted up through the gears. Passengers had to shout at one another to be heard. A convoy of these vehicles was preceded by its own din.

Despite the improvement efforts of Army engineers, the Korean roads remained narrow and maddeningly choked with civilian refugees on foot. Paved with broken rocks and pulverized by heavy military traffic, the roads coughed up a fine, calcified powder that coated vehicles and the men in them. The trip to Kyongsan could require up to half a day's driving time.

By Friday, August 25, the division's 10,000 men had been relayed from the combat zone to the rest camp.

Nothing distinguished Kyongsan and its vicinity from the rest of southern Korea. There were few structures of appropriate size and configuration for the Army to use, so the division pitched rows of tents to form its encampment. Some creeks converged in the area, allowing the men to swim or just soak their blistered feet. The location's most endearing attribute was that it was beyond the reach (if not the sound) of hostile weaponry. But there was, of course, the constant sound of cargo trucks coming and going with the division's daily provisions.

Quartermasters issued new fatigues and boots to replace worn and rotting uniforms. The men devoted time to cleaning and maintaining their weapons. Aside from these chores, most men were content to find a shady spot to stretch out on the ground, smoke cigarettes, and sleep.

Late August 1950. Kyongsan, Korea. 24th Infantry Division rest camp. The spindly trees are lombardy poplars, which the Koreans often planted in regular intervals along roadsides. *Still image from U.S. Army Signal Corps footage.*

The division's bivouac allowed the proper use of latrines and field kitchens. Hot meals were more frequent, providing a welcome break from the monotony of C-rations. The men even enjoyed occasional rations of American beer, served in individual cans that they wrapped in wet cloth so that the contents were chilled by evaporative action.

Over the next week, Philip Hughes often awoke to the smell of coffee, an aroma that he immediately associated with Tom and Wilhelmina's morning routine in their Rehoboth Beach cottage.

<<◇>>

Like every other military encampment in Korea, the Kyongsan bivouac attracted displaced civilians. By settling on the outskirts of the camp, refugees managed to feed and clothe themselves with American cast-offs and refuse. In turn, the Americans often employed the Koreans to assist with construction, cleaning, and other menial tasks. It was not unusual at the camp to see Koreans clad in over-sized Army dungarees – dutifully shining boots, washing cooking utensils, or providing haircuts.

Prostitutes began plying their trade within the vicinity. Among the 24th Division's personnel were men that not only patronized these services, but also pilfered tents and other materials to abet the trade. The division's medical companies would eventually deal with the consequences.

Medical personnel were already busy at Kyongsan. In addition to addressing any lingering battle injuries, the medical staff treated men for the chronic diseases that debilitated so many of them. Philip learned from a routine physical exam that he lost 20 pounds in just under two months. Positively diagnosed with dysentery, he suffered the classic symptoms of dry mouth, skin, and lips, along with lower abdominal soreness. The doctors may have prescribed an amoebicidal drug to rid him of intestinal parasites. Proper treatment could cure him in as little as ten days.

The Army's *Stars and Stripes* newspaper was a popular diversion. The paper's Japan bureau cranked out dailies that were usually a couple days old by the time they reached field units in Korea. *Stars and Stripes* provided updates on the war as well as news, sports, and comics from home.

Another diversion was the U.S. Armed Forces Radio Network. But just as the Army could broadcast Sinatra, Rosemary Clooney, and other musical selections from a station in Pusan, an alternative was offered by the North Koreans. "Seoul City Sue" made periodic broadcasts from the overrun capital city of South Korea.

Sue's program mixed dreamy music with motherly-voiced, English-language admonitions to any Americans who dared to wage war against the North Korean People's Army. To her listeners' chagrin, Sue would rattle off the names of American dead that were abandoned before the encroaching NKPA. Sue's impeccable English was attributed to her Arkansas origins. Born as Anna Wallis, she was a Christian missionary and teacher married to a Korean named Suh Kyoon Chul. She failed to vacate Seoul prior to the NKPA invasion, and may or may not have taken on her broadcasting duties under duress.

Mail from home caught up with the division at Kyongsan. Incoming letters and parcels were dumped in sacks before a service company tent, where clerks sorted them for subsequent distribution to regiment, then company, then platoon. The arrival of mail was truly a random event, thanks to the intricacies of trans-Pacific shipment. Items addressed to a soldier in the field needed to show only his name and divisional APO (Army Post Office) number. It was the Army's responsibility to track the whereabouts of the division and route its incoming mail accordingly. At best, it took seven days for a piece of mail to travel between the U.S. and Korea.

Because the division was resting well behind battle lines, mail could be safely announced by a bugle call. Soldiers responded in double-time. They gathered around a corporal who, much like an auctioneer, held up each piece one at a time, barking out the last name of the recipient. When hearing his name, the recipient's elation could not be overstated.

Mail from home was more than a piece of paper. A document with familiar handwriting was the soldier's most tangible connection to all that was safe, comforting, and sane. Photos and local newspaper clippings often accompanied the letters. The soldier dutifully protected these treasured documents by tucking them into his helmet liner, allowing him the joy of retrieving the same letter over and over again.

During his time in Korea, Philip Hughes wrote home repeatedly to his mother. His standard stationary was the air letter, a blue sheet of paper with adhesive tabs that, when folded properly, became its own envelope. When circumstances denied him access to stationary, Philip may have created improvised post cards as other soldiers did, tearing a panel from a C-ration carton. Because he was in a theater of war, Philip had no postage costs. He simply wrote the word "free" on the item in the same space where one would affix a postage stamp.

More than a news update, letters from a soldier at war were proof of life. Philip understood this. Despite his history with Wilhelmina, Philip clearly wished to manage his mother's emotions. His letters referred to the mundane events of daily life in the Army, as well as his aspirations. Philip was anxious to resume his education, and he anticipated doing so in the Army.

Like most other soldiers, Philip avoided the specifics of combat in his letters. On one occasion, he reflected on the war in an oblique way that suggested a nascent spiritualism:

*If hell is any worse than this, I want to stay away from it.*

Tuesday, August 29, 1950 was a gorgeous day in Korea with clear, blue skies and winds that provided welcome relief from the summer's humidity. On that day, Philip Hughes wrote what would be his last letter home. By this time, he had been in Korea for eight weeks. With the requisite optimism of a boy soldier wishing to ease his mother's concerns, Philip commented on the progress of the war, stating that "the worst appeared to be over" and that he expected "easy sailing" from then on.

Philip paused as he wrote to consider his many friends consumed by the war. Without referring directly to his combat experience, Philip was certainly shaken by the battles at Taejon and the Naktong Bulge. Still, he had not yet become totally numb to death and suffering. As breezes licked the stationary, Philip added another passage that reveals selflessness, empathy, and faith in salvation:

*Do me a favor, Mom. Pray for all the boys who were killed.*

188

In making this request, Philip invoked an imitation of *Hail Mary*, the traditional Catholic prayer of intercession. But instead of petitioning the Virgin Mary to deliver his prayer to the Almighty, Philip essentially asked the same of Wilhelmina. In all likelihood, neither Philip nor his mother noted the coincidence. Only now is the irony apparent: Wilhelmina, who projected her Catholic obligations onto her son, had one of the holiest of roles cast onto herself instead.

<<<>>>

On August 31, Philip Hughes noted his 18th birthday. He enjoyed this milestone in the comparative luxury of the Kyongsan rest camp. Nothing indicates that he announced this to his colleagues. Was there a celebration? Teenage soldiers – especially those who emerged together from the crucible of war – could easily transform one boy's birthday party into a mutual celebration of life itself. Fortified by rounds of barely chilled beer, the boys may have sung to Philip the same way they did in grammar school just a few years earlier:

> *Happy birthday to you,*
> *Happy birthday to you!*
> *Happy birthday dear Philip...*

Wholly cognizant of what they had endured in Korea, the boys could only laugh collectively at their uncertain future. Continuing with the same tune, they probably serenaded Philip with a crude but venerable verse steeped in Army tradition:

> *How fucked are you now?*
> *How fucked are you now?*
> *How fucked are you Philip...*

On this day capped by a beautiful sunset, what alternative did they have but to laugh? The U.S. Army lost an average of 77 men killed in action per day in 1950. Of the 1,898 men of the

34th Infantry Regiment deposited on the docks of Pusan on July 2, only 184 were still standing at the end of August. The rest were killed, captured, or evacuated with debilitating wounds or diseases.

From an original roster of about 140 men, Philip's Baker Company lost 49 men killed in action prior to the bivouac at Kyongsan. At least 32 of these men were killed on July 20 on the outskirts of Taejon.

1951. Korea. Unidentified, young American soldiers during a reprieve from combat. The fourth man from the left shoulders a .30-caliber light machine gun with a flash suppressor on the end of the muzzle. Each man appears to be holding a treat – birthday cake, perhaps? Their fates are unknown. *http://zoewrenchhistory.weebly.com/gallery.*

Sergeant Charles Stevenson, the Washingtonian, was among those declared missing in action after the battle in and around Taejon. He had spent less than a week in Korea. It wasn't until November that Marie Stevenson was informed by telegram that her son was missing. The delay was because the 24th Division lost so many of its headquarters staff in Taejon – including the very troops responsible for clerical duties. It took the Army weeks to reconstruct the 24th's personnel rosters.

Even with replacements, the 24th Division was still understrength, and General Walker still needed these men on the perimeter.

Keenly aware of the depleted effectiveness of the regiments within the 24th, he ordered a unit reorganization. As of September 1, 1950, the 34th Infantry Regiment was officially disbanded. Its roster was divided and transferred to the 24th Division's two remaining regiments, the 19th and the 21st. The transfer was achieved on paper while Philip and his colleagues were still encamped at Kyongsan.

Accordingly, Philip Hughes was one of the 110 enlisted men of Baker Company, 1st Battalion, 34th Regiment who became K (King) Company, 3rd Battalion, 19th Infantry Regiment.

Raymond Johnsen, now promoted to Captain, assumed command of the new K Company.

CHAPTER 28

# Hill 300

Holy Mary, Mother of God, pray for us sinners now and
at the hour of our death. *Final passage of "Hail Mary,"
the traditional Catholic prayer, per the Catechism of the
Council of Trent, 1566.*

First Lieutenant Thomas C. Clare probably didn't mind
being in uniform again. But he certainly was not pleased
to be in Korea. Tom was an Army re-tread, that is, a
veteran of the "big war" who maintained his commission as a
reservist. Hailing from a tiny crossroads town in upstate New
York, Tom enlisted in March 1942 and was quickly tapped for
officer candidate school. Sent overseas, he earned a combat
infantryman's badge before returning home to his accounting
work.

In 1947, the Defense Department decided to retroactively
upgrade service awards by issuing a Bronze Star medal to Tom
and thousands of other World War II veterans who had actually
been in combat. Save for that experience, Tom's post-war reserve
status required little of his attention. With the advent of the
Korean War, all that suddenly changed.

Now age 35, Tom Clare was about ten years older than most
first lieutenants. But no matter, the Army was losing platoon
leaders at a prodigious rate in Korea. There was an urgent need
for experienced leaders like Tom, so like many other reservists,
he received notice of his mobilization. He had precious little time
to get his personal affairs in order before flying to Japan and
quickly thereafter to Korea.

Once in Korea, Tom's first task was to catch up to the 24th
Division. Aside from disbanding and shuffling its regimental
rosters, the 24th continued to absorb replacement troops from the

states. Tom's arrival in the war zone was not too soon. On September 4, the North Korean People's Army was amassing new pressure on the Pusan Perimeter's northern frontier, just inland from the east coast. Forces of the South Korean (ROK) Capital Division held the line there, but their grip was loosening.

The NKPA continued to exploit gaps in the perimeter by moving on foot through trackless mountain passes, continuing their proven tactic of outflanking then cutting off defensive strongpoints. An enemy breakthrough would threaten Kyongju, which featured a railyard that supported the Pusan Perimeter's northern frontier. Control of Kyongju also provided access to the small but useful port at P'ohang-dong. While it had little in the way of transshipment infrastructure, the port could accommodate landing ships (LSTs) that disgorged cargo directly to the beach from their bow ramps.

General Walker had to counter the NKPA threat, but with what? All his assets in-theater were already in contact with the enemy along the entire perimeter. He had no choice but to recall the 24th Infantry Division from its rest camp.

The 24th Division would require two days, September 5 and 6, to shuttle its men and equipment almost down to Pusan, then northward on the Route 1 coastal highway. The pleasant weather of late August yielded to overcast skies and intermittent rain, which spoiled much of the ride.

The 24th would pass though the rail junction at Kyongju, and then north through the mountains outlining the Hyongsan River valley. There, the highway and a narrow-gauge railway continued north in the direction of An'gang-ni, hugging the river most of the way. An'gang-ni was already in enemy hands, and the NKPA was encroaching southwards toward Kyongju.

Among the American assets pouring into Korea were tanks and artillery to be added to the defense of the Kyongju railyard. U.S. Army personnel augmented the indigenous rail services, employing the railroad's tiny switcher locomotives to haul boxcars of ammunition up the Hyongsan valley. The same rolling stock would retrieve dead and wounded soldiers.

Wrecked, burned out trucks and equipment lost by the ROK forces along Route 1 above Kyongju were evidence of NKPA incursion over previous days. Tom Clare, Philip Hughes, and their colleagues were not pleased to see this. Still, the ROKs were hanging on to its section of the perimeter, ever so barely. The hills and valleys to the west were in question.

Lieutenant Colonel Red Ayres, the veteran of every engagement since P'yongt'aek, continued his battalion leadership position, now with the 19th Regiment. Like the men under his command, Ayres benefitted from the previous two-week rest at Kyongsan. September 6 found him back at work, planning the disposition of his command even as those ranks were still absorbing Tom Clare and other replacements. He perused maps in search of the high ground that had to be held if the valley were to remain in friendly hands.

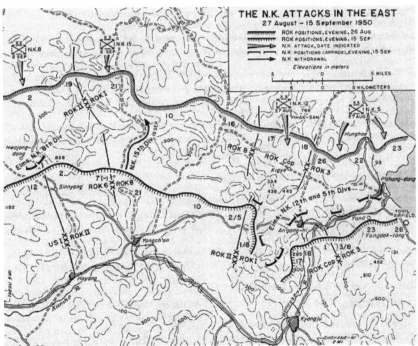

Battle of Kyongju. Philip Hughes's unit (3rd battalion, 19th Regiment) was ordered on September 5, 1950 to support the ROK Capital division's defensive front. Note location of Hill 300, lower right, between Kyongju and An'gang-ni. *U.S. Army.*

By convention, the Army documented hills by their elevation from sea level, denoted in meters. Ayres identified two key hills on the western side of the valley, about half way between Kyongju and An'gang-ni. One was Hill 285. The other, Hill 300 just to the south, became his objective.

<<<>>>

Early September marked the end of the scorching Korean summer. The nights became successively cooler. On September 8, typhoon winds from the Sea of Japan began blasting South Korea's eastern coast, bringing rain that would not let up for three days. It was amidst these blustery conditions that the U.S. Eighth Army sought to fortify the Pusan Perimeter above Kyongju.

On Friday, September 8, Ayres spread his battalion along the east-west ridge line that defined Hill 300. The line's western flank, farthest away from the Hyongsan valley, was assigned to Captain Raymond Johnsen's King Company. Along with Tom Clare and the rest of the battalion, Philip labored up the summit's slopes.

The NKPA also wanted Hill 300, if only to deny the Americans of its tactical advantage. Shortly after midnight on September 9, about 100 enemy troops emerged from the rain to knock King Company off its position. Even as the Americans skidded down the rain-swept hillside to regroup at the bottom, there in the middle of the night, a truck splashed up to disgorge a batch of bewildered replacement troops.

Captain Johnsen rallied the company to attempt two counterattacks that night, but at dawn, the hill was still in enemy hands. At half past noon, King Company advanced up the slopes, only to be repulsed yet again. Now, with all friendly troops off the hill, Johnsen could call for artillery to soften the enemy resistance on the summit.

Advancing again, this time at dusk, King Company finally claimed a tenuous hold on Hill 300. Once again, Johnsen put himself in harm's way as he moved along his men's firing positions, issuing direction and encouragement. He participated in the treatment and evacuation of at least some of the 17 men wounded during that action.

Aside from its elevation, Hill 300's only other notable feature was the cemetery found on one of its slopes. When ordered to dig in, some of King Company's men were forced to do so amidst the Korean gravesites. This was accomplished by dark on the evening of September 9, but the position was still subject to the enemy's mortar fire and occasional probes by their scout patrols.

July 3, 1951. Men of the 7th Infantry Regiment in Korea, advancing on a ridgeline that has been pounded by artillery, scorched by napalm, and littered with shell casings from rifle and machine-gun fire. In short, these are conditions very similar to those encountered by Philip Hughes on Hill 300. *U.S. Army.*

Even when unmolested by the enemy, the Americans' need to remain vigilant robbed them of much-needed sleep. Rain-soaked days and nights afforded the Americans little opportunity to sleep in their muddy redoubt on Hill 300. Some men made half-hearted attempts to pitch tents; others simply squatted under a poncho to catch their few hours' rest.

On September 10, during the hours before dawn, King Company's newcomers were startled by rustling and hissing sounds emanating from the downslope before them. Philip and the other "old-timers" matter-of-factly explained what was happening: the September afternoon sun baked the bodies of the enemy dead, which bloated with gasses as they decomposed. The cool night air contracted the corpses, causing the unnerving sounds.

Daytime skies over the Hyongsan valley on September 10 were thick with clouds, like cotton candy ensnared on the hilltops. NKPA forces took advantage of the cloud cover to probe King Company's positions on Hill 300, knowing that the weather shielded them from American artillery and air attack.

At dawn on Monday, September 11, the rains finally dissipated. The NKPA attacked Hill 300 in force, causing King Company to retreat from the crest at the cost of three dead. Clear weather allowed air power to tip the balance as it had so many times before in Korea. Philip and the rest of King Company watched a flight of F-80 jet fighter-bombers swoop down to blast NKPA troop concentrations on the reverse slope. The jets were followed by a flight of British Royal Navy Seafires from the aircraft carrier *H.M.S. Triumph*, then another batch of F-80s provided a third strike.

Before the smoke cleared, the task of retaking Hill 300 was passed on to ROK troops. Only after the ROKs secured crest could third battalion of the 19th Regiment scale the hill to relieve them.

Hill 300 was a mess. Along with 257 NKPA dead were their abandoned armaments, much of it of U.S. manufacture. Hill 300 took a rising toll on Ayres's third battalion. Philip's King Company alone lost two men killed on September 9, five more the next day, and three more on the 11th. Some of these men, like Philip, were survivors of the disbanded 34th Regiment. Their time in the Kyongsan rest camp was quickly fading from memory.

A seven-mile gap in the defensive line lay to the west of Hill 300 and the Hyongsan valley. The gap encompassed some of the most rugged terrain in South Korea. Inhabitants were scant and roads were non-existent. The wrinkled, brushy hills were traversed by a few ox trails, but these were not suitable for mechanized transport. Supplies and communications would be difficult for any army to maintain in this area.

For military purposes, the seven-mile gap was a no-man's land.

Such terrain was merely an inconvenience to troops moving on foot, as long as their armament was limited to what they could carry. Opposing troops deployed in this manner would find it difficult to seize and hold ground. They could, however, observe and harass each other. The NKPA, by virtue of its off-road mobility, was ideally prepared to conduct this aspect of warfare.

Captain Johnsen organized a patrol to monitor the area west of Hill 300 regardless of the difficult landscape and the mixed experience of the men under his command. A patrol was typically tasked to a group of eight to 12 men. The object of a reconnaissance (recon) patrol was to observe and record enemy presence and movement, then to report these findings back to upper command. It would be even more helpful if the patrol captured an enemy soldier or two and brought them back for questioning. A successful patrol required a mix of speed, stealth, and keen awareness of one's surroundings.

Johnsen's plans for the mission were straightforward: a two-prong patrol would encircle an area immediately west of Hill 300. To perform this task, Johnsen selected two patrol leaders who in turn would pick their own troop detail. One leader would be 28-year-old 2nd Lieutenant Billy McCarver from Abilene, Texas. Johnsen had high confidence in McCarver, who fought every step of the way through Korea ever since arriving on July 3.

Staffing the other team presented a problem. It was not ideal to entrust a patrol – especially a recon patrol – to a new man, but the attrition of junior officers left Johnsen with no alternative. For leading the second detail, he tapped the newly-arrived Lieutenant Tom Clare.

McCarver's detail would head north then west, while Clare's group headed west then north. After meeting at an appointed time, the united patrol would then return to Johnsen's command post with their findings.

Tom Clare immediately assembled a squad from his platoon. Some of these men, but not all, were true riflemen. Others were replacements who had arrived at the front as recently as the night of September 8-9. These included clerks and other rear-echelon types who had not fired a weapon since basic training. The "old hands" would have to give the newcomers a quick refresher on how to handle a rifle and its ammunition.

Included in Lieutenant Clare's squad were Private Don Eugene Gibson, age 18, from Zillah, Washington; and Corporal Akeji "Norman" Morinaga, age 25, from Honolulu, Hawaii. Morinaga was a Japanese American who originally enlisted during World War II and was sent to Ft. Snelling, Minnesota to train as an interpreter. After the war, he continued in the Army and was managing a quartermaster's warehouse in Japan when he was reassigned to Korea.

There was also Corporal Fred Harvey Myers, age 21, from Comanche, Oklahoma. He was a clerk by training. Both Myers and Morinaga were stationed in Japan during the occupation, where each had found a Japanese bride. By 1950, each already had a young son.

Among the others joining them was Private Philip Hughes, an 18-year-old from Washington, D.C. This kid was among the few survivors of the 34th Regiment. He contrasted sharply with the clean, well-fed replacements. His frame was made scrawny by dysentery, yet Hughes had survived ten weeks of constant deployment in the field without a scratch. He got cleaned up a bit during the Kyongsan bivouac, but that was more than a week ago. His complexion had become tan and leathery, the result of extended exposure to the summer sun. Philip's wispy teenager beard had returned. His sun-bleached hair was already getting shaggy again.

Lieutenant Clare did not know – nor did he need to know – that Philip Hughes was once an orphan, groomed throughout his childhood to become a priest. Nor did he know that Philip was a high school dropout and runaway, eventually committed to reform school. None of this was of concern to the U.S. Army embattled on Hill 300 or anywhere else on the Pusan Perimeter. For Lieutenant Clare's purposes, Hughes was among the most combat-experienced troops available in King Company. He would be an asset on the patrol.

Indeed, Philip had gone on plenty of patrols. The Kum River line. Koch'ang. The Naktong Bulge. Lots of walking – up, down, and around the hills. Enemy contact was very often insignificant, if at all. Any hostility usually involved a brief exchange of fire over a great distance.

The alternative was to stay on Hill 300 to consolidate its encampment. Dig a latrine. Collect fallen comrades while burying the remains of the enemy. As tired as he was, Philip probably welcomed the patrol as a reprieve from the foul stench of filth and death.

For Philip Hughes, the patrol would be the latest in the series of journeys that propelled his life.

The date was Tuesday, September 12. The skies were clearing now, presenting a vista unlike any Philip had seen before in Korea. From the summit of Hill 300, he could look to the east where the sky met the Sea of Japan. With an unobstructed view of the horizon, he could detect the curvature of the earth. Philip could trace LSTs from the port of P'ohang-dong making their way out to sea – approaching, meeting, then crossing the horizon as they dwindled completely from sight.

This patrol would be a foray into the late summer foliage, where high grass shielded a chorus of crickets. In the bushes were cicadas, issuing an undulating whirring sound, somewhat like a sewing machine in dire need of lubrication. In the overgrown, remote terrain west of Hill 300, the insect noise could generate over 100 decibels of volume, masking the sound of any soldier's approach, whether friend or foe.

The sound was familiar to Philip. There was little to distinguish the late summer sounds of Korea from those behind the dunes of Rehoboth Beach… or the playground of Turkey Thicket.

The men lit up cigarettes while Lieutenant Clare knelt to scratch a map of their mission in the dirt. Like the others, Philip

Hughes strapped on one of those uncomfortable web cartridge belts with clips for his M1 rifle. Then he retrieved two or three hand grenades from a wooden crate, pinning these on his tunic. He grabbed a water canteen and plopped a halazone tablet in it.

Lieutenants Clare and McCarver synchronized their wrist watches and nodded to each other in a parting gesture. The smokers each took one last draw on their cigarettes before stamping them out in the dirt. Proceeding in a line, leaving about ten paces between each other, the two squads advanced into no-man's land.

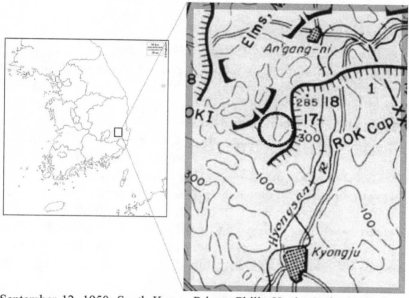

September 12, 1950. South Korea. Private Philip Hughes's fatal patrol was conducted in the "no-man's land" immediately west of Hill 300, depicted by the circled area in the inset.

# CHAPTER 29

# Western Union

Washington, D.C. was unexpectedly chilly on Sunday, September 24, 1950. The high temperature that day reached only 58 degrees, whereas the previous day's high was 73. The cold front brought clear skies with winds gusting up to 25 miles per hour.

The Hughes family attended Mass that morning at St. Anthony's. Frank Hughes was 16 now, out of reform school and back home with his parents in Brookland. He was a sophomore at Bell Vocational High School and had a load of homework spread across the dining room table.

Frank heard car doors snap shut in front of the house, and thought nothing of it. But from a front window, Wilhelmina saw an olive-green sedan with a white star and the words "U.S. ARMY" stenciled on the side. A man and a woman, both in dress uniforms, approached the front door. The woman clutched a zippered portfolio in one hand while she held her hat in place with the other. The male officer was probably a chaplain, perhaps even a Catholic. Wilhelmina immediately knew why they were there.

She stepped outside on the front step while Frank hovered in the doorway. The female officer presented a Western Union telegram, an eight by five-and-one-half inch document.

Slowly, Wilhelmina seated herself on the cold cement of the top step; the female officer then did the same. Nobody had details about the circumstances of Philip's death. At this point in the war, they could not provide insight regarding the repatriation of remains or subsequent funeral arrangements.

The chaplain could offer a prayer. That was about it. Wilhelmina had not yet begun to process the news she had received so stoically.

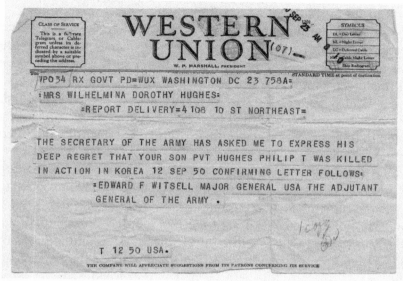

*Courtesy of the Hughes family.*

Staff writers from both *The Washington Post* and *The Washington Evening Star* routinely scanned Defense Department casualty lists as soon as they were published. They looked for the names of soldiers from "the District area," which included Washington, D.C. and the nearby counties of Maryland and Virginia. On Monday, the day after the telegram was delivered, one reporter from each paper descended on the Hugheses' residence.

The result was two remarkably similar articles, one published by the *Star* on Monday, September 25, and the other published on the next day by the *Post*. Both included a three-quarter portrait of Philip in dress uniform and close-cropped hair under a peaked cap. He was described as the 15th District-area man killed in Korea.

With her subsequent weekdays all to herself, Wilhelmina had more than enough time to ruminate over Philip's loss. She could not yet fathom the gap in continuity: she had received Philip's last letter on September 10, and now he was ...*dead*? She longed for an explanation to fill that gap.

Sheer frustration motivated Wilhelmina to investigate on her own. She had all of Washington, D.C. at her disposal, but where would she start? Phone calls to the Defense Department were ultimately useless. Her last resort would be a longshot: to visit the patient wards at what was then Walter Reed General Hospital, the Army's flagship medical facility, located in upper Northwest D.C. Sooner or later she would have to encounter someone who knew her son.

By the end of September 1950, Washington, D.C.'s Bolling Air Force Base received up to three large transport planes per day loaded with Korean War casualties bound for Walter Reed. With over 1,100 beds, the 113-acre facility focused on occupational therapy for men whose battle injuries resulted in amputations or other long-term incapacities. Wilhelmina scanned the newspaper for lists of war casualties received at Walter Reed.

She made multiple uptown trips on the Georgia Avenue streetcar line to visit the hospital, usually bringing a tin of cookies for goodwill. Her sleuthing was an iterative process. She learned very quickly that there was little use in asking "*Did you know Philip Hughes?*" Instead, she focused on unit affiliations. This was no small feat, given the reassignments and unit reorganizations within the 24th Infantry Division.

Her diligence eventually paid off. One day, she found a boy from the 19th Infantry Regiment at Walter Reed. This young man was recuperating from a shot clean through the hip. *Philip Hughes... yes, the kid who arm-wrestled everyone.* "We liked him."

*So what happened to him?* The area was Hill 300, near Kyongju. There was a pincer movement. One team headed north, the other to the west. Philip was with the west-bound squad. They were in an open field. NKPA troops fired down upon them from an elevated position. The ambush wiped out Philip and his team.

Tom Clare's patrol was ambushed just three days short of September 15. On that date, 40,000 soldiers and marines conducted an amphibious invasion at Inchon, far to the north, near Seoul. With the threat of being cut off from their supplies, those NKPA troops on the Pusan Perimeter fell into a rout within days. This allowed the United Nations forces to advance the liberation of South Korea. Private Philip Hughes, one of the first boy soldiers committed to the Korean War, managed to survive all but the last few days of the near-suicidal defense of the Pusan Perimeter.

<<<>>>

There is no detailed accounting of the fate of Lieutenant Clare and his squad on Hill 300. A few scattered facts make an incomplete picture.

King Company of the 19th Infantry Regiment submitted a morning report for September 12, 1950 indicating 12 men "missing in action." Eight of the MIAs were subsequently found to be alive and returned to duty within the next couple of days. However, Lieutenant Thomas Clare's status changed from MIA to "killed in action" on September 14. The status of Corporals Morinaga and Myers was also changed from MIA to KIA on September 15. Private Don Gibson's MIA status was not reverted to KIA before September 17.

Private Philip Thomas Hughes was unique among the day's casualties in that he never held the interim status of "missing." The morning report for September 12 directly changes his status from "on duty" to KIA.

The National Archives' definitive casualty database for the Korean War, created in 1979, reconciles contemporary records from 1950. The Archives database shows that Clare, Morinaga, Myers, Gibson, and Philip Hughes were all killed in action on September 12.

Wilhelmina was *told* that Philip participated in the ill-fated patrol. What if the young soldier in Walter Reed Hospital was mistaken? There is nothing to verify that all 12 of the MIAs were members of that patrol.

The death of Philip Thomas Hughes is recorded on this microfilm image of the September 12, 1950 Morning Report, K Company, 19th Infantry Regiment, U.S. Army 24th Division. *National Personnel Records Center, U.S. National Archives.*

Another piece of the puzzle comes from Lieutenant Billy McCarver, leader of the second patrol. In late October 1950, *The New York Times* told his story in an article by war correspondent Charles Grutzner. McCarver was recognized as a former prisoner of war who escaped from the North Koreans after about two weeks of captivity. He described his capture as the consequence of his conducting a patrol on September 12 near P'ohang (not far from Kyongju). Most of his squad was captured because they waited too long in a prescribed spot waiting for another patrol that *failed to arrive at the appointed time*. McCarver's name also appears on the July 3, 1950 morning report for Baker Company of the 34th Regiment – the same unit that would become King

Company of the 19th. This is the circumstantial basis for linking Billy McCarver's patrol to that of Tom Clare.

If Philip Hughes really was a participant in Tom Clare's patrol, his final disposition is still a matter of conjecture. That the remains of Tom Clare and his men were identified over a span of several days suggests two possible explanations.

In one scenario, the patrol was scattered by the ambush so that the men did not perish in close proximity to each other. The second scenario is that the fallen were all retrieved at the same time, but the remains of some were so badly shot up that positive identification was delayed. After all, by September 12, the 19th Regiment's third battalion had developed a backlog of remains awaiting graves registration.

If the first man to fall in the ambush was killed instantly, he was the luckiest because he never knew what hit him. Conversely, the others had several terrifying seconds to muster a reaction: fight or flee? Philip's remains were the first to be found. What does that say about his location in the squad, or how far he might have fled once the ambush was underway?

Philip Hughes's luck had not completely failed him. That his body was retrieved on the same day that he fell meant – maybe – that the NKPA troops lost the opportunity to defile his remains. There is a certain dignity accruing to a soldier who dies with his boots on.

So Philip was no longer subject to combat. A combat soldier's tour of duty in Korea was from nine to 12 months, depending on rotation points earned. Given Philip's arrival in July 1950, he would not be due for rotation until at least April 1951.

His subsequent travels with King Company in the fall and winter of 1950 would have taken him across the 38th parallel into North Korea, where American forces had to fight in sub-zero temperatures to escape a trap set by the surprise intervention of the Chinese People's Volunteer Army. The 19th Regiment would suffer tremendous losses in the spring offensive as the Chinese pushed the battle lines back into South Korea.

Death also precluded his capture. By September 16, 1950, 401 American combatants were confirmed as captured by North

Korean forces, with another 2,107 counted as missing. Many captive soldiers perished during the course of forced marches and mass executions before they even reached the wretched prison camps in the far corners of North Korea. Some were mistakenly killed by their own artillery or air strikes while in captivity.

Overall, some 7,100 Americans were taken prisoner in Korea, 40 percent of whom died in captivity. When captives were exchanged upon the Korean War's cease-fire in 1953, 900 known American prisoners were not among those repatriated. Those who came home carried some combination of emotional or physical scars for the rest of their lives.

Philip was not one of the men shipped home minus one or more limbs. Nor was he rendered blind, deaf, or impotent by wounds. Philip was spared the indignity of seeking ever-diminishing health care services from a dysfunctional Veterans Administration.

About 7,800 American soldiers from the Korean War remain unaccounted for to this day. Many rest in unmarked and forgotten graves. That Philip Thomas Hughes was not left among them is the final, modest measure of his luck.

Battles raged up and down most of the Korean peninsula through late 1951. By then, the fighting coalesced on a static front aligned more or less with where it all started – at the 38th parallel. As fighting continued, the opposing nations entered into peace talks. Battles were waged not so much to gain land, but for the combatants to demonstrate their resolve relative to the negotiation process. It would take two years to craft a cease-fire that allowed both sides to save face. Meanwhile, American fighting men employed dark humor as they were reduced to pawns in the brinksmanship of contentious negotiation. *Die for a tie* became their morbid mantra. Cease-fire was finally achieved on July 27, 1953, but it has yet to become a true armistice.

Strictly speaking, the Korean War has yet to end.

<<◇>>

In early November 1950, the Hugheses received a letter from the Secretary of the Army. Given the terseness of the Western Union telegram received earlier, this correspondence was a shrewd gesture on the Army's part. As with all Hughes family matters both large and small, Wilhelmina was the point of contact.

1 November 1950

My dear Mrs. Hughes:

The President has requested me to inform you that the Purple Heart has been awarded posthumously to your son, Private Philip T. Hughes, Infantry, who sacrificed his life in Korea.

The medal, which you will receive in a short time, is of slight intrinsic value, but rich with the tradition for which Americans have so gallantly given their lives ever since the days of George Washington, whose profile and coat of arms adorn the medal.

Little that we can do or say will console you for the loss of your loved one. He has gone, however, in honor and in the company of patriots. Let me, in communicating to you the country's gratitude, also express to you its admiration for his valor and devotion.

Sincerely yours,

Frank Pace Jr

Frank Pace, Jr.
Secretary of the Army

Mrs. Wilhelmina D. Hughes,
    4108 10th Street, N. E.,
    Washington, D. C.

*Courtesy of the Hughes family.*

# CHAPTER 30

# Please Omit Flowers

The Korean War was the first war from which the remains of American personnel killed in action were retrieved during hostilities for repatriation and burial back home. This policy, however, was declared before the means to fulfill it were secured. Philip was dead, but he would have to wait before embarking on his final journey.

Personnel from King Company were tasked with retrieving the remains of their own fallen from the battlefield. Philip was first placed in an oiled canvas bag, which was then hauled on a stretcher for collection near the medical company's aid station, down the road from Hill 300 on the outskirts of Kyongju. Discretion demanded that the dead be shielded from the view of living troops.

The aid station staff began the registration process by removing grenades, ammunition belts, compasses, binoculars, and any other government property from the deceased. Pockets were sliced open with a knife, and personal effects were dutifully inventoried and placed in a bag for eventual forwarding to next of kin.

The staff created a report of interment file, the contents of which would grow through each step of processing. Like all other American military personnel, Philip Hughes wore an embossed, stainless steel dog tag with rolled edges, threaded on a ball chain worn around the neck. The tag was notched on one side to facilitate the embossing mechanism. These tags were fundamental to the administration of mortuary information.

Reading from top to bottom, the tag recorded the bearer's name, serial number, year of tetanus shot, blood type, and religious identity. Since Philip's blood type is unknown today, the letter "A" was inserted as a place-holder in this pictorial re-creation, followed by a "C" for Catholic:

The deceased soldier's dog tag was removed and stamped on all documents in the file. With these tasks accomplished, the body was sealed in the waterproof bag and set aside for subsequent removal by graves registration staff. One set of documents remained in graves registration files while the other traveled with the remains.

The 24th Infantry Division established its own temporary cemetery during the height of the Pusan Perimeter battles. Graves registration required a site with minimal slope and good drainage, free of subsurface rock. An ideal spot was provided at the Miryang Experimental Farm. Administration of the cemetery was entrusted initially to a staff of about 20 soldiers under the command of a master sergeant. Officially organized on August 23, 1950, the Miryang Cemetery already had 365 interments by that date. Another 1,026 would be added by September 7.

Like all the other plots, Philip Hughes's temporary resting place was a mound with a wooden marker at the head. To protect the identity of grave sites in case of any future interference, the burial plots were arranged in a tight, well-surveyed grid. The graves registration paperwork accompanying the body was rolled up and placed in a small glass bottle with a removable seal. This bottle was tucked under the deceased's left armpit during temporary interment.

In the meantime, the Quartermaster of the U.S. Army's Far East Command assessed the problem of transferring the deceased from temporary interment to final repatriation at home. In mid-December 1950, a single command was assembled for all Eighth Army mortuary services, which included forensic labs for certifying identities and embalming services for preserving remains for transshipment. The Army's preliminary plans for locating such activity in Korea were quickly abandoned due to a lack of proper facilities as well as the looming threat of Chinese forces that had just entered the war.

1950. Temporary cemetery somewhere in Korea. *U.S. Army, Harry S. Truman Library and Museum.*

The Army quickly settled on Camp Kokura, a former Japanese officers' barracks complex on the northern tip of Kyushu. The site included a Coca-Cola bottling plant established for the post-war occupation forces. It would take between 60 to 90 days to reconfigure and equip the facility. This would become the 8204th Army Graves Registration Service Group. The staff grew to ten officers, 51 enlisted men, and one civilian. Activity began on January 2, 1951.

By late January, disinterments began at the Miryang Cemetery. Due to the backlog of work at Kokura, however, the remains from Miryang were re-interred temporarily at Tanggok, just outside of Pusan, a site that aggregated remains from all United Nations units operating in Korea. The 8204th would not work its way through the backlog until May 1951, at which time the Army began to transfer remains from Tanggok.

Philip's remains were processed at Kokura during the summer of 1951. By this time, the staffing had grown to permit two-shift operations. The process required, by necessity, an assembly-line organization.

The first task fell to the Central Identification Lab, which examined the physical characteristics of each set of remains. This included hair color, skin pigmentation, height, tattoos, scars, shoe size, teeth, and bone and cranial formations. To generate fingerprints, the staff would first repair skin surface by injecting water or hot paraffin into the deceased's finger tissue. The technicians took fluoroscope images to document any bone malformations that could aid identification. Body and dental features were photographed; along with schematic diagrams, this information comprised a case history for comparison to each man's medical records. A Board of Officers reviewed the identification paperwork for each man.

Only after identity was certified would the remains advance to the embalming stage. This involved the injection of a hardening compound that effectively prohibited further deterioration of body tissue. The remains were then dressed and placed in caskets with identifying labels. Batches of remains were dispatched to the port every ten days. The base chaplain at Kokura was joined by chaplains of all denominations from nearby facilities to conduct a memorial service in the mausoleum area. Each casket was draped with an American flag.

The batch was loaded onto a train bound for Yokohama and escorted by an 8204th honor guard to the dock. Loading the caskets onto the ship proceeded as a solemn ceremony, featuring a military band playing *Taps* and a three-volley rifle salute. By November 1951, all the remains from the interim cemetery in Tanggok, which included Philip Hughes, had been processed.

March 11, 1951. Yokohama, Japan. Three-volley salute for the USS General George M. Randall, (AP-115) and its cargo, including the first group of American Korean War dead to be returned to the U.S. *US National Archives photo 80-G-427104.*

After the trans-Pacific crossing, which probably docked in San Francisco, Philip's remains were routed by train to New York City, the initial transshipment hub for all east coast interments. From there, his casket was forwarded to Washington, D.C. for storage at Ft. Myer, Virginia in anticipation of final burial at Arlington National Cemetery.

HUGHES, PHILIP THOMAS. Killed in Korea on September 1?. 1950. PHILIP THOMAS HUGHES. beloved son of Thomas T. and Wilhelmina Knue Hughes. brother of Francis Joseph Hughes. Other relatives also survive. Solemn high requiem mass at St. Anthony's Church. 12th and Monroe sts. n.e.. at 9 a.m. Wednesday. February ?7. Prayers and final absolution Fort Myer Chapel at 11 a.m. Interment. with full military honors. Arlington National Cemetery. Please omit flowers.                                            25

Philip Thomas Hughes's obituary. *The Washington Evening Star*, Sunday, February 24, 1952. *D.C. Public Library Washingtoniana Collection.*

Wednesday, February 27, 1952 was a mild day in Washington, D.C., with the temperature peaking at 46 degrees. Moderate winds from the north blew across the Potomac from the city and up the slopes of Arlington National Cemetery. Tom, Wilhelmina, and Frank Hughes were there for the final farewell.

Tom Clare is also buried at Arlington. So is Harold "Red" Ayres, along with his wife, Elizabeth. Across the cemetery, near its far western border, is the resting place of Charles Leroy Stevenson.

Knowing that her son was missing, his mother, Marie, waited anxiously for almost two months. As Christmas of 1950 approached, she embraced positive thinking. She purchased a new automobile and parked it in front of her home on Emerson Street, intending to give it to her son upon his return.

Her hopes were dashed when she received the worst possible news. Sergeant Stevenson's remains were found in December 1950, at the site of the clash on the Kapch'on River above Taejon. He was interred in Arlington in May 1952. Per the wishes that he had voiced years earlier, he was laid to rest near his father, a World War I veteran. Marie joined them when she passed in 1985.

<<<>>>

Philip Hughes's plot at Arlington Cemetery is number 2870, Section 12. It is located on a gentle slope that used to be the front yard of Arlington House, the pre-Civil War home of General Robert E. Lee. The front of Philip's tombstone faces due east, aligned with the Lincoln Memorial, then the Washington Monument, and finally the U.S. Capitol. A constant parade of passenger jets from Reagan National Airport fly before his gravesite, but aside from that, the location is rather peaceful.

Ironically, and perhaps fittingly, Philip's final resting place is one of many gathered in neat, institutional rows, just like the boarding school dorm, the YMCA, the reform school bunk, and the army barracks – all communal settings that echoed the orphanage of his earliest years.

2013. Arlington National Cemetery. *Photo by* Another Believer, *Wikipedia Commons.*

As is true of everyone, Philip Thomas Hughes did not choose the foundation upon which his life was built. Philip's parents, both natural and adoptive, plus the cultural tribe of Brookland, unwittingly conspired to provide that foundation. And like all of us, Philip had but one foundation upon which he made the choices that shaped the 6,586 days of his life.

By his mid-teen years, Philip became acutely aware of the dissonances imposed by the unsettling love-hate relationship with his adoptive mother. Philip's angst fueled his impulse – not for conflict, but to flee – running away from "home" in search of a life of his own choosing. This became the Battle of Turkey Thicket.

The Army at first accommodated Philip's search for freedom and identity. Yet the Army drew him inexorably into war. That war consumed him, causing him to disappear like a stone that sinks into oblivion when tossed into a pond. But like the stone cast away, Philip's death created ripples on the water of life. This is evident in the continuing story of his brother, Frank.

# CHAPTER 31

# Ripples on the Water

For to this you have been called, because
Christ also suffered for you, *leaving you an
example, so that you might follow in his
footsteps* (1 Peter 2:21).

Washington, D.C. is technically not a state, but a federal
district. As a consequence, in 1950, its residents had
no legislative representation in the U.S. Congress, the
Electoral College, or a voice in the Constitutional amendment
process. Nor were they eligible to cast popular votes in
presidential elections. Yet District residents like the Hugheses
were subject to federal taxation.

Additionally, the sons of District residents were required at
the age of 18 to register for the military draft. Despite this
obligation, Philip and his parents had no say for or against the
election of presidents who, like Harry Truman, could effectively
engage the U.S. in undeclared wars. Disenfranchisement of D.C.
citizens would not materially change until the 23rd Amendment
to the U.S. Constitution was ratified in 1961. This Amendment
was precipitated in part by legislators' awareness of the 142
District of Columbia residents who made the ultimate sacrifice
for the Korean "police action."

Having said this, what may have mattered more to Tom and
Wilhelmina Hughes was the city's changing social climate. At
ages 68 and 63, respectively in 1952, they were prepared to make
a year-round home in Rehoboth Beach. Tom was ready to retire
from the Mine Workers' union. Relocation to Rehoboth became
an attractive choice: Aside from the pleasant beach atmosphere,
Delaware's culture was not changing as quickly as it was in the
nation's capital.

<<◇>>

Tom and Wilhelmina received the standard $10,000 cash pay-out from Philip's Army life insurance policy. Wilhelmina directed some funds into real estate maintenance and others to church donations. The balance would soon be put to another very good use.

The Hugheses' property at 5 Newcastle Street in Rehoboth was ideally located near their other property holdings. It was just a stone's throw from the boardwalk and around the corner from St. Edmond's Catholic Church. They could take advantage of the Delaware school system for Frank's remaining high school years.

C. 1952. Rehoboth Beach, Delaware. *Delaware State Archives.*

Wilhelmina must have felt some measure of guilt for precipitating Philip's fate. One consequence of his death was the subsequent unravelling of Wilhelmina's aspirations for Frank. She surrendered her desire to continue her family's tradition of sending sons into the Catholic priesthood. Even if her aspirations for Frank remained the same, she knew she had to change her approach. Complicating all of this was the fact that she and Frank remained at odds, a clash of personalities that made it difficult to live under the same roof.

Wilhelmina sought alternative living arrangements for Frank. For a short time, he boarded in town at the home of one of Wilhelmina's real estate acquaintances. This ended when Frank took too many liberties with his host's automobile. The next arrangement involved a farm on the outskirts of town. Here, Frank assumed a roster of chores that began before sunrise.

Frank was enrolled in Rehoboth High School, where he left mixed impressions with the faculty. Frank's stellar academic performance, especially in mathematics, was marred by his tendency to be disruptive in class. Having had enough of these episodes, the principal arranged for Frank to pay a visit to Coach Coveleski's office.

Frank L. Coveleski was an athletics instructor with an abiding empathy for wayward boys. He was one of three children raised by his widowed mother, Olympia, in a small town in the heart of Pennsylvania's Schuylkill valley coal country. Forced to work in a textile mill at an early age, Coach knew a thing or two about being a knucklehead. At age 35 in 1952, Coach Coveleski was the captain of the Rehoboth Beach lifeguards in addition to his football and swim team instruction at the high school. He used his influence to set boys straight.

The Coach summoned young Frank Hughes to his office. Frank slouched against the door jamb.

*Have a seat*, Coach insisted.

Frank refused.

*Sit down*, the Coach snapped.

After that inauspicious beginning, Frank was invited to join the football team. Camaraderie fostered with the coach and his teammates made a lasting impact on Frank Hughes. Through steady encouragement, Coach Coveleski saw to it that Frank focused his talents productively. Frank would say years later that this was a pivotal experience in his life.

Frank Hughes graduated from high school in 1953 and spent that summer at the beach. When he wasn't training to be a lifeguard, Frank paraded the boardwalk like all the other kids. He often found his father perched in one of the boardwalk gazebos.

Tom Hughes was adjusting to retirement, increasingly seeking comfort in alcohol. He may have suffered from depression. On one of these chance encounters, Frank found Tom weepy, and sat with him. Never before had Tom engaged Frank in a conversation of any depth. There on the boardwalk of Rehoboth Beach, he did so for the first time.

Frank made periodic visits to Wilhelmina that summer. In hindsight, it was clear that Wilhelmina had been doing a *lot* of thinking, pondering Philip's death, Frank's future, and her own role in shaping both.

On one visit, Frank told her that his immediate plans were to continue working on the farm. She responded: *I have a better idea.* Although she had never owned – and would never own – an automobile of her own, Wilhelmina offered to buy Frank a car so that he could tour the country. He accepted, so Wilhelmina tapped her nest egg accordingly. Frank would spend most of the next two years on the road, returning to Rehoboth for the summers to work as a lifeguard with Coach Coveleski.

Frank remembers covering all the lower 48 states in his journeys, wearing out an Oldsmobile and then a Lincoln Capri. If his travels rivaled those described in Jack Kerouac's classic *On the Road*, we'll never know. He remains circumspect about those days. Frank did reveal that his preferred rest stop would be a library where he could pursue his fascination with theoretical mathematics.

Frank found himself one day in the Stanford University library in Palo Alto, California. He approached the reference desk to request a text on structural analysis by the famed faculty member Stephen Timoshenko. The librarian responded that Frank could actually meet Dr. Timoshenko, who just so happened to be standing right there next to him.

This chance meeting put Frank Hughes on a stellar career track. Dr. Timochenko introduced Frank to a faculty connection at Florida's University of Miami. Within short order, Frank would enroll there to pursue a Bachelor of Science in Engineering. Wilhelmina showed her support by purchasing a little house for him just off campus. After finishing undergraduate studies in 1960, he went to George Washington University in Washington, D.C., where his master's study examined theoretical and applied mathematics.

Frank stayed in the Washington area. He flourished professionally, starting at the National Security Agency. In 1962, he joined IBM, which granted him a sabbatical to pursue doctoral work at George Washington University. Frank then became part of IBM's support team for the Goddard Space Flight Center in 1966.

Meanwhile, through the 1960s, Frank made periodic excursions to Rehoboth Beach to visit Tom and Wilhelmina. It was there that Frank met Florence "Cici" Dewey. The vivacious daughter of U.S. Army General Lawrence Russell Dewey, Cici was educated at the Sorbonne in Paris. She pursued Frank, but it took him a while to realize that she was *the one.*

1965. Washington, D.C. Frank Hughes. *Courtesy of the Hughes family.*

Frank's parents adjusted to their golden years of retirement. Wilhelmina kept busy with her portfolio of rental properties, and of course, the church. Tom became active in the community, if only to routinely chat up business owners on the boardwalk. At one point, someone suggested that Tom should run for mayor of Rehoboth Beach, but it came to naught.

Having treated themselves to a television set, the Hugheses watched nightly news depictions of young American soldiers dispatched to another far-east Asian war, this one in a place called "Vietnam."

They remembered Philip.

<<<>>>

On Tuesday, March 12, 1968, Tom and Wilhelmina started their daily routine in Rehoboth Beach when each settled into a chair with their newspapers. It was one of those raw, late-winter days with intermittent rain and snow. Ships in the Delaware Bay would sound a foghorn every so often. As always, Wilhelmina took a break to make a pot of coffee.

When she returned, Tom, the blue-eyed Scotsman, was dead.

Wilhelmina held on for another year, just long enough for Frank to tell her about his intended bride. Now in a nursing home, Wilhelmina wanted to know only one thing.

*What church does she belong to?*

Frank and Cici knew this question awaited them. They chose the truth: Cici was raised in the Episcopal church. Wilhelmina refused to meet her.

On May 14, 1969, Wilhelmina died, and was buried beside Tom just outside Dover, Delaware. Tom and Wilhelmina never saw Frank's wife, his daughter, or his granddaughter.

<<<>>>

Frank's career continued with a succession of executive appointments, both in government and in private industry. His resume includes a stop as an Assistant Postmaster General during the Lyndon Johnson administration. He was one of a group of young, hand-picked, private-sector executives tasked with bringing business processes to the postal service.

In the 1980s, he accepted an executive director position with a bank in Australia. To accommodate this move, he put many household possessions into storage. The storage facility sustained a water leak while he was away, compromising some valuables that he was forced to discard. Among these were Philip Hughes's letters, photos, and other personal effects retrieved from Korea.

In the last stage of his career, Frank Hughes taught an entire generation of analysts at the National Defense Intelligence College. His daughter grew up to become a professor of veterinary medicine. As of this writing, Frank and Cici live comfortably in Washington, D.C.

The Battle of Turkey Thicket is over. It ended when Frank Hughes pulled out of Rehoboth Beach behind the wheel of his Oldsmobile. A uniquely gifted man, Frank thrived with God's grace. Without it, he could have easily succumbed to a life of dysfunction. Frank won the battle, but his victory came at his brother's expense. There's a palpable poetic justice that allowed Philip Thomas Hughes – the boy who so loved to travel – to provide the final measure of his life to finance Frank's ensuing journeys of self-discovery. Had it not been for Philip Thomas Hughes's sacrifice, his mother may never have seen the futility of imposing her will on her adopted sons. We may wonder if Frank, without that freedom, would have flourished as he did.

Frank has since renewed his pursuit of Catholicism. In so doing, he joins a community of individuals bound in spirit, each of whom builds their faith one day at a time.

# Epilogue

Baltimore, Maryland
March 2017

My family enjoys the beach. We started going to Rehoboth, Delaware around 1995 and have done so almost every year since. First, it was just my wife and me, then we included our daughter after she was born in 2000. We usually spend a week there, including a Sunday, where we'll attend St. Edmond's Catholic Church, one block from the boardwalk.

The Masses at St. Edmond's are crowded during the summer, when the locals are joined by visitors from throughout the mid-Atlantic region. The current chapel, dedicated in 1940, now features French provincial design cues in its interior. Its vaulted ceiling, paneled with knotty pine planks, conveys warmth and charm.

Receiving communion during Mass at St. Edmond's involves lining up in the center aisle to approach the altar, then returning to one's pew via the side passageways. In doing this, year after year, I took notice of a spindle-cut plaque, bolted to the wainscot of the right interior wall, opposite the front row of pews. About the size of an automobile license plate, it is the only one of its kind in the entire church.

This stuck with me for several reasons. My leisure reading leans toward military history, including many texts about the Korean War. Here was a memorial to one of its victims, a mere kid. Given only the information on the plaque, I knew immediately that Philip Thomas Hughes was involved in the darkest, most brutal days of that conflict.

As a father, I could only guess how his parents assuaged their grief by investing in this modest plaque. It saddened me to think that 50-plus years later, visitors paraded by this plaque every

Sunday in their tee-shirts, shorts, and flip-flops, oblivious to the identity of this boy and the sacrifice he made.

*Author's collection.*

My curiosity grew with the advent of the Internet. Year by year, the amount of available information grew, allowing me to reconstruct this kid's identity. Searchable databases of Korean War casualties appeared online. The old newspaper articles provided his photograph and quotes from his last letter home. It's through these words that the ghost of Philip Thomas Hughes speaks to us today.

From public information alone, I found that Philip and I shared many similarities. We were both born in Washington, D.C. Our first childhood homes were built around the same time, each located near the remains of one of the Civil War forts that once protected the nation's capital – Fort Bunker Hill in Philip's case, Fort Slocum in my case. I lived just over two miles from the Hugheses' residence on 10th Street.

Philip and I both spent some time at a school in Canada. We shared a connection with Rehoboth Beach. Philip was Catholic by upbringing, whereas I am by choice.

Assembling this narrative was an exercise in scouring published histories plus the granular data found in vital statistics. These were matched with first-person testimonies. Finding the latter was a race against time to contact men who were on the ground in Korea at the same time as Philip Hughes. Sadly, I was often too late. I never got to speak with Lloyd Pate (1933-2013),

Ralph Derr Harrity (1923-2013), or Uzal Ent (1927-2015). Fortunately, these men left priceless memoirs. The observations of Will Hill Tankersley (1928-2015) would have been added, but he passed only days before I attempted to call him.

The real breakthrough in my investigation came in October 2014. The name *Philip Thomas Hughes* appeared on a recently-created genealogy webpage. I emailed the page administrator, who I soon found out was Frank Hughes's daughter. Think about it: in this age of Internet phishing and email scams, Frank and his family took a big leap of faith in responding to me. First, there was an email. This was followed by a very pleasant phone call with Frank and Cici, in which I learned about the adoption, the expectation of priesthood, and the runaway episode. Of all the people in the world, Frank is probably the only person still alive who has an active recollection of Philip's life and circumstances.

I felt that this could make an interesting book (and I hope it did).

August 2016. Washington, D.C. Frank and Cici Hughes. *Author's collection.*

In very short order, my wife and I met with Frank and Cici for lunch at their favorite restaurant. Unprompted, the staff brought Cici her usual drink just as we were seated at a booth.

Then, reaching into her purse, she produced two electronic candles and placed these on the table next to the bread sticks. I have remained charmed by the Hugheses ever since that moment.

Unfailingly gracious, Frank and Cici met with me several times over the next couple of years. I conducted interviews with Frank and discussed the draft of this book. It was slow going, due to my professional commitments.

Time has dulled Frank's memories, but we unearthed little gems with each subsequent discussion. His oral history was complemented by facts presented in books, journal articles, and nuggets mined from the Internet. Intending all along that this should be a true story, I refrained from conjecture until the conclusion of this epilogue. A few episodes were condensed, hopefully reducing narrative clutter.

When visiting the Hugheses in February 2017, Cici produced the very same 48-star U.S. flag, folded in tri-corner fashion, that once adorned Philip's casket prior to his interment at Arlington. By touching its fabric, I reached out across the decades. That's as close as I will ever get to Philip Thomas Hughes.

Being from different eras, and different "tribes," as it were, Philip and I came of age in vastly dissimilar societies. While I am thoroughly fascinated by his story, this book is the only connection that he and I could ever possibly have. *To everything there is a season, and a time to every purpose under heaven.*

If he had survived, Philip Hughes would have been 84 years old as I write this. He might have noted with great interest the development of South Korea into a free and prosperous society, knowing that he contributed to that nation's good fortunes.

Philip may have joined the many Korean War veterans who chose in their later years to revisit the battlefields where they once fought and lost friends so long ago. Economic progress has since obliterated many of these sites. The port city of Pusan is dense with modern construction, much of it vertical, and buzzing with activity.

Baker Company's position east of the road above P'yongt'aek is now the site of the SsangYong Motor Company's sprawling assembly plant. At Taejon, a low-rise residential suburb covers the space where Baker Company backed the front line of Red Ayres's battalion behind the Kapch'on River. Just across the highway to the south, where Ayres's command post was overrun, a water treatment plant stands today. His southbound avenue of withdrawal, to the west of Taejon, features a series of huge apartment buildings built where the rice paddies once dominated the flats. The ridges remain largely undeveloped, owing to their steepness, and forests have regenerated on these slopes.

The rugged landscape of the Naktong Bulge enjoys a similar reprieve. Finally, Hill 300 and the no-man's land west of the Hyongsan valley also remain largely undeveloped. Trees now obscure the path on which Tom Clare's patrol was ambushed on September 12, 1950.

Return on the investment for the lives of Philip Hughes and his allied combatants is effectively depicted by a striking satellite image of the Korean peninsula at night. North and South Korea are in dramatic contrast by the volume of artificial light they produce.

*www.northkoreatech.org*

How could Philip not be moved by seeing the outcome to which he contributed? He could have visited the Korean War Veterans' Memorial in Washington, D.C., admiring its 19 stainless steel statues and seeing his reflection in the polished granite wall.

Philip would also have witnessed momentous changes to the city in which he grew up. Like so many of the Brookland families of his era, Philip would have quit the District to take up residence in suburban Maryland or Virginia. People tended to scatter radially outward from the center of the city, so folks from Northeast Washington wound up in Maryland towns like Greenbelt, Bowie, or Laurel.

Turkey Thicket is still in Brookland, host to an eponymous recreation center and the Brookland Middle School, both of modern construction with state-of-the-art technologies and amenities. Philip Hughes, the boy who so often rode to adventure by train, would be amused to know that railroad-themed play structures are installed in Turkey Thicket's recreation center. There's also a baseball field and tennis courts that provide the spirit of open space that defined Turkey Thicket from its beginning.

Finally – while there's no way to know for certain – it's quite possible that a woman in Japan, now in her late eighties, privately recalls the late spring of 1950 and the 17-year-old American boy with whom she shared her most intimate affections.

<<<◇>>>

I asked Frank what he thought Philip might have done with his life. Reflecting on the tough, high school drop-out, Frank could only wince in response. Philip probably could not match Frank's intellectual firepower. But he certainly had a heart. Philip was not extraordinarily close to his little brother, but he naturally assumed the role of Frank's protector. I could easily see Philip pursuing a career in law enforcement. In the Washington, D.C. area, he would have many jurisdictions from which to choose, plus the U.S. Park Police, the Capitol Police, and perhaps even the U.S. Secret Service.

Philip would have been fascinated by a Catholic – John F. Kennedy – ascending to the White House. He would witness the end of streetcars and advent of the Metrorail system that replaced them. Philip would resent the riots and protests of the late 1960s, yet be in awe of the city's subsequent commercial and demographic metamorphosis that continues today.

Philip would drive cars built in Detroit with plenty of steel and chrome, tuning the radio to WMAL's Harden and Weaver morning show, or perhaps Felix Grant's late-night jazz program. He would buy lumber from Hechingers, and watch Washington area housing values soar during the 1970s. He would note the demolition of Griffith Stadium and its replacement by what would become RFK Stadium, followed by Fedex Field and Nationals Park. I suspect Philip would have cheered the Washington Redskins football teams just as I did.

Frank and Philip would each have their pick of a beach cottage from Wilhelmina's estate. Their families would gather in Rehoboth on Newcastle Street each summer through the 1970s, 80s, and later, perhaps even today. And as all grandfathers seem to do, they would have some fabulous stories to tell their grandkids.

Plot 2870, Section 12,
Arlington National Cemetery.
*ANC website.*

# Technical Note 1
## Explanation of U.S. Army Unit Organization and Leadership Ranks

Private Philip Hughes's U.S. Army organizational assignment in Korea can be described as follows:

| July 2 – August 31, 1950 | September 1-12, 1950 |
|---|---|
| U.S. Eighth Army, 24th Division, 34th Regiment, 1st Battalion, B (Baker) Company. | U.S. Eighth Army, 24th Division, 19th Regiment, 3rd Battalion, K (King) Company. |

His chain of command while assigned to the 34th Infantry Regiment (July-August 1950) is shown here:

| UNIT | COMMANDER (Age in 1950) | PERIOD OF COMMAND | CAUSE OF TERMINATION |
|---|---|---|---|
| U.S. Eighth Army | Lt. Gen. Walton H. Walker (60) | 1948-23 Dec 1950 | Died, vehicle accident |
| 24th Infantry Division | Maj. Gen. William F. Dean (50) | Oct 1949-21 Jul 1950 | Captured/POW, released July 1953 |
| 34th Infantry Regiment | Col. Jay B. Lovless (49) <br> Col. Robert R. Martin (48) <br> Col. Robert L. "Pappy" Wadlington (49) <br> Col. Charles E. Beauchamp (42) | Mar 1950–7 Jul 1950 <br> 7-8 Jul 1950 <br> 8-16 Jul 1950 <br> 16 Jul-31 Aug 1950 | Relieved per Dean <br> Killed in action <br> Temporary <br> Reassigned to 32/IR, 7/ID |
| 1st Battalion | Lt. Col. Lawrence G. Paulus (46) <br> Lt. Col. Harold "Red" Ayres (31) | 1949? - 4 Jul 1950 <br> 4 Jul – 31 Aug 1950 | Relieved per Dean <br> Transferred to 3/19 IR |
| B Company | 1st Lt. Raymond K. Johnsen (31) | 2 Jul?-31 Aug 1950 | Transferred to 3/19 IR |

There are no surviving records to indicate Philip Hughes's platoon or squad affiliations.

To appreciate unit designations, think of the Army in 1950 as comparable to a manufacturing organization of the same era. As a rifleman holding the rank of "private," Philip Hughes would be equivalent to a worker on an assembly line: one of many individuals who follows orders to carry out the work of the organization. To continue the comparison:

• The company is equivalent to a single manufacturing plant site. The company's C.O. (that's *see-oh* for "commanding officer") typically holds the rank of captain, or sometimes, a First Lieutenant. Think of the C.O. as equivalent to a plant manager. The C.O., in this case 1st Lt. (later Captain) Raymond K. Johnsen, was the highest ranking officer with whom a private like Philip would have regular contact.

• A single manufacturing plant site usually hosts multiple process lines. The Army equivalent would be the company's platoons, each led by a lieutenant or a master sergeant.

• Multiple plant sites may be managed as a region. Similarly, multiple companies are organized as a battalion. A battalion is commanded by a lieutenant colonel or a major. Philip's Baker Company (later, King Company) was one of three companies constituting the battalion commanded by Lt. Col. Harold "Red" Ayres.

• Three battalions made up a regiment, just as the manufacturer compiles several regions into a business unit. A colonel leads a regiment. Red Ayres's command was the first battalion of the 34th Infantry Regiment, led by a series of commanders during Philip's tenure in Korea.

• Three regiments made up a division, just as business units make up a corporation. A division is headed by a major general. The 34th Infantry Regiment accrued to the 24th Infantry Division, initially commanded by Maj. General William F. Dean.

• Finally, the Eighth Army, led by Lieutenant General Walton H. Walker, bound together four infantry divisions. The Eighth Army was equivalent to a holding company that united four corporations.

# Technical Note 2
## Documentation of Philip Thomas Hughes's Military Service

On July 12, 1973, the National Personnel Records Center of the U.S. National Archives, located in St. Louis, Missouri, suffered a disastrous fire. This event destroyed the service records for up to 18 million Army personnel discharged between 1912 and 1960. Among the records destroyed were those of Philip Thomas Hughes. Facts pertaining to his Army career can be reconstructed using secondary data, which for this text includes the following:

**Newspaper articles.** Newspaper articles about Philip Hughes ran on September 25 (*The Washington Evening Star*) and September 26 (*The Washington Post*), 1950. Reporters for both papers interviewed his mother, Wilhelmina. The articles are remarkably similar, but each provides a couple of facts not revealed in the other. The *Star* article affirms that Philip enlisted in November 1949. Both papers affirm that he returned to his home in Washington, D.C. for a 20-day furlough in April, that he then went to Japan, and that he had arrived in Korea with the 24th Infantry Division in July 1950. Both articles are available from the digitized Washingtoniana collection of the D.C. Public Library.

**Western Union Telegram.** The Hughes family archive contains an original Western Union Telegram addressed to Wilhelmina Hughes, date-stamped September 23, 1950. It announces that "PVT HUGHES PHILIP T WAS KILLED IN ACTION IN KOREA 12 SEP 50..." Note that all Defense Department records, including Philip's tombstone inscription, indicate his holding the rank of "private." By exception, *The Washington Post* and *Evening Star* newspapers described him as a "private first class" (PFC).

**The U.S. National Archives'** Defense Casualty Analysis System generated by 2008 an electronic database of Korean War casualties. This is available online. Each casualty is described by name, rank, serial number, dates of birth and death, state of residence, military occupation, and last unit assignment. This database describes Philip Hughes as being from Washington, D.C., and as a private (grade E-2) assigned to King company of the 19th Infantry Regiment (abbreviated per traditional military practice as "K/19").

**Morning report archives.** Army units at the company level generate morning reports – a daily accounting of personnel present, missing, or absent with reason. Fortunately, morning reports from the Korean War (while not 100 percent intact) are currently available on microfilm at the National Archives facility in St. Louis, Missouri. The September 12, 1950 morning report for K/19 exists today on microfilm. It reports a change in status for Philip Thomas Hughes from "DY" (on duty) to "KIA" (killed in action).

**Scholarly articles and publications.** History shows that the third Battalion of the 19th Infantry Regiment was reconstituted from paper status on September 1, 1950. Initial staffing of 3/19 was achieved by receiving survivors of the 34th Regiment's first battalion, as follows:

| 34th Infantry Regiment, First Battalion July 2 – August 31, 1950 | | 19th Infantry Regiment, Third Battalion September 1, 1950 and later |
|---|---|---|
| Headquarters Company | → | Headquarters Company |
| A (Able) Company | → | I (Item) Company* |
| B (Baker) Company | → | K (King) Company |
| C (Charlie) Company | → | L (Love) Company |

*The U.S. Army does not designate a "J" (Jay) Company simply because the capital letters "J" and "I" are too similar in appearance, fostering possible confusion in written documents.

Given that Philip Hughes arrived in Korea in July, the above strongly suggests that his original assignment was to Baker

Company of the 34th Infantry Regiment. The history of the 34th – from P'yongt'aek to Ch'onan, Taejon, and the Pusan Perimeter – provides the probable itinerary for Philip's travels in Korea. His arrival could have been one of five dates: (1) July 2, when the 34th disembarked from the *Takasago Maru* in Pusan; (2) July 4, when the 34th received transfers from the 35th Infantry Regiment at the Pusan train station; (3) on or about July 18, when the 34th received replacements at its position on the Kapch'on River line; (4) July 23, when replacements were added to the ranks after the tragic battle and withdrawal from Taejon, or (5) July 30, when the regiment received 75 enlisted men and officers at Kwanbin-ni.

Note, however, that *The Washington Post* and *Evening Star* newspaper articles reference a letter that Philip wrote to his mother on August 29, 1950, in which he indicated losing 20 pounds to dysentery and related exertion. As he wrote that letter, Philip had seen no combat since August 20. He had, however, participated in field operations from August 5-20, but in locations on the Pusan Perimeter that received (comparatively) good logistics support. Such dramatic weight loss would have taken some time, while the onset of dysentery would likely coincide with exposure to contaminated water supplies. This suggests that Philip participated in the Battle of Taejon at the Kapch'on River, including the July 20-23 cross-country straggling episode with fellow survivors of that battle.

**Hughes family oral history.** Among the personal effects sent home to Philip Hughes's family was a photograph of his Japanese girlfriend. Clearly, Philip spent some time in Japan prior to going to Korea. His initial unit affiliation in Japan is not certain, as he could have been assigned to the 34th Infantry Regiment from the start, or transferred in from another division.

The narrative of this text recounts the 34th Regiment's experience in Korea from its initial arrival on July 2, 1950. Philip Hughes may or may not have been with the unit as it engaged the enemy at P'yongt'aek on July 6 or Ch'onan on July 7-8. It's very likely that he was involved in the action on the Kum River line (July 13-14) and Taejon (July 20). When I interviewed Frank

Hughes, he recalled that Philip was "at Taejon," which would place him with Baker Company on the Kapch'on River line under Raymond Johnsen's command. In recounting the 34th's action, this text's narrative only implies (rather than affirms) Philip's involvement prior to July 20, 1950. The dramatic story of these earliest engagements attempts to convey the rude and fearsome initiation to battle from the perspective of any young infantryman. Hopefully, then, this narrative gives voice not only to Philip, but to all the boys who sacrificed their lives in the brutal war in Korea.

C. 1950. Korea. Young and confident, a group of U.S. Army soldiers pose in front of a GMC "deuce-and-a-half" truck, so named for its 2.5 ton (rated) cargo-carrying capacity. The identities and fates of these men are unknown. *U.S. Army.*

236

# Technical Note 3
## Map: Philip Hughes's Korean War

Landmarks from Philip Hughes's service in Korea. He arrived in Korea "in July" 1950. He *may* have been at P'yongt'aek and Ch'onan; he was *probably* at Taejon and Yosu; and was certainly at all the other sites shown here except Seoul, the capital of South Korea. Note that place names shown here are spelled as they would have been in 1950, using the pre-2000 romanization standard for translation of the Korean (Hangeul) language.

# Technical Note 4
## Philip Hughes's Comrades in Arms

PVT EDWARD
MORRISON
Age 19
KIA P'yongt'aek

PVT JACKIE LEE
MURDOCK
Age 17
POW P'yongt'aek
Died in Captivity

SGT ALFRED
BLOTZ
Age 33
KIA Taejon

PFC BEUFORD
McCOMAS
Age 21
KIA Taejon

CPL CLARENCE
PRUETT
Age 20
KIA Taejon

CPL NEIL
SATHER
Age 28
KIA Taejon

PFC CHARLES SKERO
Age 20
POW Taejon
Died in Captivity

SGT CHARLES
LEROY STEVENSON
Age 26
KIA Taejon

SFC BENJAMIN
MILLIKEN
Age 27
KIA Kwanbin-ni

SGT JAMES
CASH
Age 32
KIA Naktong Bulge

PFC RONALD
McKENZIE
Age 21
KIA Naktong Bulge

SGT HOMER
SPRANKLE
Age 18
KIA Naktong Bulge

MSG SAMUEL
EDWARD SCOTT
Age 25
KIA Kyongju, Hill 300

CPL AKEJI "NORMAN"
MORINAGA
Age 25
KIA Kyongju, Hill 300

PFC LOUIS
ULRICH
Age 20
MIA 23 Apr 1951

A sampling of U.S. Army enlisted men whose unit and location assignments in Korea coincided with those of Philip Hughes. He probably knew at least some of these young men. All but Morinaga were with Baker Company, 34th Infantry Regiment; Morinaga would join King Company, 19th Infantry Regiment, to which Hughes, Scott, and Ulrich had already been transferred after the 34th Regiment was disbanded on September 1, 1950. The losses at P'yongt'aek were sustained July 6, 1950; Taejon, July 20; Kwanbin-ni, July 30; Naktong Bulge, August 8-12; and Hill 300, September 9-12. *POW* – prisoner of war. *KIA* – killed in action. *MIA* – missing in action.

238